Forever Haunted

DUTCHIE MALLOY

authorHOUSE®

AuthorHouse™
1663 Liberty Drive
Bloomington, IN 47403
www.authorhouse.com
Phone: 1 (800) 839-8640

Published by AuthorHouse   02/16/2016

ISBN: 978-1-5049-7391-5 (sc)
ISBN: 978-1-5049-7392-2 (e)

CONTENTS

DEDICATION

This book is dedicated to my best friend, my loving husband and father of my children who left this world way to soon but will never be forgotten. My loving sister and my beautiful niece also leaving this world way to premature and leaving emptiness in our hearts and unrest in our souls. My Grandfather and for all lost souls trying to find their way home. My mother who always believed in me, but would never admit she too had a gift. One she didn't understand and didn't want to! I know she has a lot of secrets of her own. Sadly her stories will never be told, as she refuses to speak of them to this day.

My friends Marci, Kristyn, and Joyce. Who believed in me when no one else did, and I could never forget Donna. A very special person that has also gone long before she should have. She probably understood me more than anyone ever came close enough. We would talk about the many crazy things that I had encountered in my adult life. Funny how she seemed to relate to these things and yet, I still did not confide in her of the many things from childhood. Maybe I didn't think she would believe it. It's really to bad, I miss our talks and now that memories have unfolded, she may have been able to help me uncover the missing pieces.

Marci and Kristyn have stood by me trying to make my life more bearable when things got weird. Joyce has taken the initiative to try and help me rationalize my life, but in the end it is what it is. She set my mind at ease when she researched the mantis man. I was so thrilled to discover others had also witnessed his presence as well as other creatures. So it wasn't a child's imagination after all! My friends are the best and they like me regardless of what they will discover about me. I know I can count on them, they have my back. I can't thank them enough, for always being there for me.

Of course I couldn't leave out my beautiful grandchildren, Cierra, Chyanne and Cameron whom have had to endure all the craziness over the years! Not to mention having to live in my overcrowded home with all our ghost, that often scares the crap out of them!

Funny they want to be with me anyway! They too have had their share of paranormal activities, plagued with the same curse or dare I say gift as myself. They were so excited when I told them I was writing my memories, they too encouraged me, they probably think I'm crazy, but they still love me! And last but not least my two sons for not having me committed. Even though sometimes I had doubts of my own sanity. Reluctantly they also have had their share in the paranormal!

Special thanks to Kaitlin and Russell, for their patience and tolerance while I was writing this disaster! They patiently, guided me smacking my hands as I kept hitting enter and double space thru this entire process! All the while silently cursing under their breath! Ha! At last my disaster has come to pass, hope you like it! Thank you for all your help, love you!

PREFACE

Forever Haunted is a collection of true stories based from memories of my childhood and on into my adult life. It is based on the paranormal, a subject many people still refuse to acknowledge!

I realize some of these stories will have eyes rolling in disbelief, some will say what a crock of shit so farfetched, stupid and unbelievable. Well I can't blame them, heck I was there and I was that kid and I wouldn't have believed them either had I not actually experienced them myself! They have stayed fresh in my mind all these years, like it or not I have to accept it.

Yes it is true I had an imagination when I was a child. I have searched my mind trying to rationalize the things that I have experienced, the things I have seen and the situations I was put in. Sometimes I think it would be so much easier if I could blame it on my imagination! However, the memories are too vivid, to clear to dismiss. I have to accept the truth and I seek to find the answers.

This book has been written in hopes that someone out there may have encountered the same experiences, or even crossed the same path that I have. It is in search of the truth and trying to make sense of my crazy mixed up life. My life is a giant puzzle with many missing pieces. Someone out there may have a missing piece that will make sense and fit into the empty spaces. I may have a piece of their puzzled life as well.

The fact that you chose to read this book has already created some kind of connection. Memories are sometimes hidden in the back of our minds for safe keeping. They sometimes protect us from things we are not ready to understand. Sometimes they lay in wait until just the right moment.

I always said someday I would write a book, problem was I didn't know where to start. I surprised myself when I finally started writing and one memory uncovered another, then another.

Memories at the time I thought I would never forget, tucked away yet hidden for safe keeping until now. There they were plain as the day they occurred. So vivid it was like stepping back in time, yet standing still.

Memories of surroundings as well as events overwhelmed me. It wasn't like I was just remembering them or seeing myself as in a dream, but I was somehow that child again. Reliving the past that collided with the present. I could smell the flowers and the rain, I could hear the thunder and see the flashes of fury, I could touch things long past as if I were experiencing them all over again!

It's about discovery, searching, reaching for answers. It's about understanding and coming to grips as to what I am, and where I go from here. Who knows where our paths will lead us? Who knows where we will be and what we will experience along the way through life's journey. Some people plan their lives while others lives are planned for them. For some of us are marked for whatever reason from the time we enter this world our destinies are planned for us. In the end did we really have a choice?

IN THE BEGINNING

It was a bitter cold February night in the darkened hills of West Virginia, everything was frozen over from the harsh cold winds and snow covered ground. I can symphonize with the reluctance of anyone not wanting to venture out on a night like that, especially on foot. The wind and the hail mixed with the snow adding to the already treacherous ice below made it hard to see, and unbearable to travel! I guess one could say I started off on the wrong foot right away with my father. After all he was the lucky one that had to go for the Doctor. The snow was high on the mountain and the ice was treacherous, it would be a difficult journey down and more difficult coming up again.

Maybe I was not meant to be but somehow I survived without any real brain damage or birth defect, although, some may argue about the brain thing. The cord of life linking me to the world I clung to and the world I was thrust into was wrapped tightly around my neck. The air the new world supplied was not meant for me. My body blue and lifeless. So near to death. It would have been easier for her to let me go. They didn't need another mouth to feed.

The panic she must have felt, the aloneness and desperation must have been overwhelming. Still she fought to keep me. My aunt watched in horror as my mother desperately grabbed at the cord. All the knowledge of life and the world I most surely possessed at that moment, lay in limbo. Life and death so near to each other.

If I had died I would have taken the knowledge and secrets of the universe that I would miss out on with me. But I lived and the knowledge that flooded me at birth was lost to me. Only to gain back a small portion through experience and my journey through life!

I believe what God gives, God can take away. But, not without leaving you something. The part of me that was almost taken that night, made a way for my journey. To experience what most do not believe in, to shape and mold me. To make me understand in a way that would forever haunt me. The strength and drive and quest for answers would haunt me. My guides through many disguises would open doors for me. They would protect me along the way. Would she have wanted me, had she known what I was or would become? Perhaps she did know, maybe that's why she fought so hard to keep me.

My Grandfather waited patiently in the other room caring for three other siblings, helpless in what else to do. Something at the window captured my grandfather's attention. A slight peck, then another following several others, growing louder. The frozen window couldn't with stand much more, my Grandfather slightly opened the window trying to make it stop when a red bird flew into the room.

Old folklore suggests that a bird entering a house is the sign of a potential death. This was cause for alarm as my aunts horror grew louder. In a sense, the folk lore almost proved it's point. My Grandfather captured the bird and waited for the worst.

The cry came and echoed through the house as I aggressively took in the air, then cradled in the safety of my mother's arms, it was clear I wanted to be here. After all she had fought so hard to keep me. So the force that held me so tightly let me go. Hence, therefore I became who I am today, still as unsure I belong here as the day I was born. And to think it all started with the will to survive and love from the other side or perhaps both sides. One that wanted to keep me, the other not wanting to let go!

I sometimes have strange thoughts, the part of me that escaped death, my true self, can't help but wonder, for maybe it was with them that I really belonged. As I felt I never quite fit in anywhere.

As it turned out I wasn't the only survivor that night, oddly enough the red bird also survived and lived a full year in captivity growing stronger each day. In fact a year later the bird was given to the doctor as payment for delivering my baby brother. Ironically it lived long after that. My mother had delivered me so the doctor's work was done by the time they reached the house. My dad although half frozen to death survived as well, cursing the day I was born! Luckily the heat from the fireplace and a hot cup of coffee was a welcome payment for the Doctor that night. He named the bird "Destiny."

Maybe somehow he knew I was different than the others. Maybe he could sense my destiny, maybe he knew I was marked. Maybe he knew from the beginning I would be "Haunted Forever."

MY LOVE OF CRITTERS

As I grew from year to year I guess I was always a bit different. I kept things to myself and was rather quiet and shy. I played with cats and bugs and hopping things. I loved catching fireflies and putting them in a jar. I would watch them for long periods of time. I often would fall asleep, mesmerized by the twinkling lights coming from within the jar.

I guess my favorite was the praying mantis. I would run down the hill with an old mason jar the holes already poked into the top by my Papaw. I would hold out my finger as the mighty mantis world climb up and sit there. I thought he was beautiful and from royalty.

His wings became his royal robe and on his head he wore a crown. His eyes were large and seemed to look inside my soul, I would bow and call him my "King." His army was the many grasshoppers than jumped ever so high in the field. I would gather as many as I could and put them inside the jar. I would pretend enemy soldiers were approaching, I would shake the jar just enough to get them ready to fight! I carefully unscrewed the lid, gave it one last shake and turned the aggressive grasshoppers lose to protect "Our King!"

I seemed to have some kind of weirdness about critters and bugs, but bats seemed to like me a lot more than I liked them! Although I wasn't afraid of them when I was young, I avoided them as much as possible when I got older. As I recall I had had more than my share of encounters with them over the years.

I recall when I was maybe three or four years old. My mother was standing in the dining room ironing as she so often did. My brothers and sisters were in the bedroom watching television. I'm not sure why I was in the living room on the couch unless I was bad as I often was.

I know it was very late, I was just sitting there watching something fly around the room. It would swoop down and soar up and then down again. I watched it for a while. I could hear the flapping of its wings. It wasn't really all that big. I know that because I was little and I remember holding out my finger and it perched on my finger. I was fascinated by it, its eyes were so big and black as it stared into mine. I said "Mommy, look at the pretty bird!"

I sure didn't expect what happened next! She had a horrible look on her face as she ran towards me! I had never seen my gentle loving Mommy look like that! I couldn't tell if she was mad at me or scared, but she didn't look like my Mommy at that moment!

She grabbed a broom in the nearby corner in the kitchen as she ran at me! I flinched when she came closer, she swatted at the birdie as I screamed "Mommy, my birdie!" In a instance I was off the couch in her arms as "My birdie" flew into the air, diving up and down as she ran to the bedroom and practically threw me in, saying "Stay there!" I don't remember crying it happened so fast.

I kept thinking my poor little birdie, why doesn't she like him! I saw the car lights out the window and a few minutes later the door opened, my dad was home. I heard lots of noises coming from the living room. A loud squeaking or screeching sound I had never heard before. I being so curious opened the door just enough to peek out when I saw my dad hit "My birdie!" knocking it to the floor!

I ran out the door as I saw him hold it down with the broom and to my horror pressed his lit cigarette into to eye of "My Birdie!" I didn't understand. He never even met my birdie, so why didn't he like him? A tear ran down my cheek as I stood there not able to move.

My Mommy told me my birdie was bad, and I should never try and touch or play with any of them again. She said my birdie was dangerous and if it bit me it could give me a disease and maybe kill me! I looked at my precious little Birdie, so little and helpless. How could it be so bad?!

In my journey thru life I could never fathom that a few years later I would not only see, but witness the biggest red eyed bat, and the chaos it left behind ever imaginable!

I remember when I was living in California the strange little alien creature that sat on my step. He was pink, and looked as though he was naked and he certainly didn't look like any bug I had ever seen and have never seen another since.

It just sat there with its huge dark eyes, legs crossed like he was quiet comfortable, he wasn't afraid when I knelt in front of it to get a better look. It was probably at least a good five inches tall. He cocked his head to get a better look at me. His mouth reminded me of that of a turtle and seemed to smile back at me.

I thought there was a little recognition in his eyes of the mighty mantis although he looked nothing like "My King." I turned my head just briefly and when I turned back, he was gone! He didn't have wings and there wasn't anywhere he could have gotten to so fast that I wouldn't have seen him as he went. Yet, he had just seemed to vanish. I searched books for a picture of the strange creature but found nothing that looked like it.

The reason this has all come to my mind is somehow something to do with my destiny. Perhaps I was not meant to be here and somehow managed to slip into this realm. Knowing things were going to happen or knowing what someone was going to say or do before they said or did it. Warnings that have come from time to time and then the animals that seemed to come to our house just to die!

I sometimes could see things others couldn't, I felt things and never understood them. Places I recognized but had never been there before. Getting confused when I saw or knew something that happened before it happened sometimes years before, Sometimes I would feel guilty that I didn't "Warn people," but I thought it had already happened! The lists just goes on and on. Let's face it, I was weird then and the older I get the crazier the situations and life collide making things more unique and complicated! So many missing pieces yet one by one they are starting to appear.

I have seen the faces of evil, yet, not been blinded by it!
I have walked into evil, yet, not become it!
I have experienced the wrath of evil, but not given in to it!
I have seen many things hard to explain, yet, I haven't given up!
I know goodness surrounds me, yet I can't grasp it!
I know darkness follows me, yet I can't escape it!
Leaving me alone and forever haunted!

THE MANTIS MAN

I walked in my sleep as a child and my dad would get very angry with me. We lived across the street from the river and the large river rats would invade our house regardless of the cats in the neighborhood. It was on one of these sleep walks that I first seen the man in the basement.

I must have wandered down into the darkness of the basement, I remember waking up and was a little frightened, I wasn't sure why I was down there and it was so dark. There was a slight light that shown from the kitchen upstairs that traced the outline of the steps. I was afraid of the rats that seemed to be everywhere and when I started for the stairs I saw him!

He was very tall his face reminded me of my mantis with large dark eyes. He wore a kind of cloak or western duster like the cowboys wore on television. He just stood looking at me. In my child mind I thought of him as being a threat to my king as he was so much larger.

I hurried up the stairs and jumped back into bed. Peeking out from the covers I watched the doorway hoping he wouldn't be there. I knew I couldn't tell that he was there, because I would just get into trouble for "Stirring up the rats!"

I thought I had perhaps dreamed it all as when I awoke the next day to the sun coming in and the darkness was again no threat. However a part of me that just had to see for myself, once again ventured back into the basement. I remember the damp smell as I carefully stepped down ever so quietly.

I took one step at a time being ever so cautious, even though the light was on it was still fairly dark I was thankful for the sunlight filtering thru the basement windows casting a glow to help light my way. I reached the bottom of the stairs and chanced stepping onto the cold dark ground that was our basement floor.

I looked around to make sure there were no rats running around, once satisfied I peered into the corner beside the furnace where I had first laid eyes on him. He stood there not moving, his eyes large and dark just as I had seen a few hours before. He was real! He said not a word, and although I didn't tell when I saw him the first time, I knew I would not tell on him now. He held his finger to his lips as if to tell me be quiet! Suddenly I wasn't afraid, but I really don't know why.

My dad used to call me crazy as I would play with cats more than dolls or other girl toys, I would dress them in dolls clothes and push them in my little buggy all around the house. One day I guess he was just mad at me but I don't know why. It's funny that I don't remember what I could have done to make him so mad. I was playing with my cat in the buggy and when I came around the corner by the back door he was standing there.

He grabbed my cat and put a rope around her neck, tied her to the door knob and started beating her with his belt! My Papaw the one I could always count on was there and tried to make him stop. I cried and begged and pleaded with him to stop! He just looked at me with such hate and continued hitting at her as she cried out and ran with what little rope she had to avoid the strikes!

Then I saw him, in the daylight, tall, big and dark like a huge shadow behind my dad! He looked scary, but I wasn't afraid. I looked at him, it was at that moment I wanted him to rip my dad's head off and throw it into the river!!

He just stood there behind him, looking at me. I felt so helpless and truly alone. I thought he was my friend! We held a secret, together, a trust a bond! I didn't understand why he didn't stop him!

My papaw must have seen him, but he never said anything. He was trying to make my dad stop. Finally he did stop and when he did, he put my cat in an old flour sack and tied the top. As I reached for it, he shoved me down and headed across the street to the river!

I wasn't allowed to cross the street. I was never allowed to go near the river. I didn't care I ran after him crying. "Please, please don't hurt my cat!" My pleas fell on deaf ears.

Down the hill he went with me following as fast as I could. At the edge of the water he swung my cat around his head several times. I could hear my cat's frantic cries as he threw my beloved cat into the cold dark river without a chance of survival!

I stood there shaking and crying and I never knew what hate was until that very moment! The Mantis Man now, nowhere to be seen. I stood there alone as I helplessly watched, the tears dried on my face and I vowed he would never make me cry, never, ever again!

We returned from the river, for the first time he seemed to acknowledge me, stared at me, with cold dead eyes, void of any human emotion. Not a hint of remorse. I stared back, not blinking, and tried to see into the soul of the devil, I called dad.

My Papaw had passed out in the back yard with his wine bottle cradled under his arm. My dad took the whiskey bottle from inside his shirt took a long drink, spilling some down the corners of his mouth and onto his shirt. He kicked the door open and left me standing outside.

I only saw the Mantis Man one other time after that, my friend Nick and I were playing down the hill in back of the neighbors yard. It was starting to get dark and I knew I was going to be in trouble because I had snuck out to catch fireflies.

A storm had suddenly appeared from the summer sky. The burst of thunder shook the ground as lighting lite up the earth. We started running for the house as the cold rain fell from the menacing sky above. The dark clouds seemed to grow arms as each bolt of lighting threatened to grab me and pull me into the darkness! A swarm of bats seemed to circle us a few times almost like they were confused at the sudden change in the weather.

We ran past the garage when I remembered my fireflies! My precious fireflies trapped inside that old mason jar. I turned and ran down the hill splashing thru puddles of cold water and mud. I grabbed my jar and raced back up the hill. The bats now seemed to chase me as I ran.

The rain was coming down so hard now I could hardly see. The wire clothes line was hanging very low and I ran right into it knocking me to the ground. I felt the sting of the wire cut across my eyelids as I laid there in the mud.

The Mantis Man stood behind my mother as she ran out to get me. The lighting crashed and the thunder roared. My eyes had small slits across my eyelids and my vision was slightly blurry. I turned at the doorway to see where he had gone, before I could catch a glimpse of him one last time my mom shut the door.

I had dropped my precious fireflies when I fell and in all the confusion I had forgotten all about them I was exhausted and cold as I lay snuggled in the blankets. One last burst of lighting light up the darkness. I could see the Mantis Man at my window, he put his finger once again to his lips and then he was gone.

I awoke some time later and felt something beside me in the bed I shared with my sister. It was hard and I could feel its coldness against my stomach. I pulled down the covers although the jar was veiled in smudges of dried mud it glowed beside me! I couldn't believe what I saw! My precious fireflies, I smiled when I thought of the Mantis Man for I knew it was he who had carried them into the house out of the storm. I never saw him again after that dark stormy night so long ago.

A day or so later, I got the surprise of my life! I had just came home from school, I had just started Kindergarten. Something jumped out from behind the kitchen stove! I couldn't believe it! My poor Precious, drowned, beaten, old dead cat was back!!! So, it was true! I had always heard a cat had nine lives and I swore I would protect it from the eight more lives it would have!

Could this have also been the work of the Mantis Man? I knew it was my cat, not a duplicate, as she let me dress her, and sing to her, and push her around the yard in my little buggy! She had a few whelps on her back from the struggle and the beating she took. Yet, here she was! She was bound so tightly and beaten so badly, the river was so cold, dark and deep, how else could she have gotten out?!

Maybe it was his way of preparing me for what was to come throughout my life. Making me tough enough to handle the things I would encounter. Whatever, he had in mind I will never forget him.

Maybe he wasn't able to stop my dad, maybe even though he was big, he was as helpless as I was. I know I will never forget him and his kindness. I know in his own way he protected me. Perhaps his mission was complete, he did what he came to do. He gave me insight, I learned to trust and I could see thru the eyes of evil, as young as I was, I gained strength and a hard core, building my foundation preparing for the next chapter in my life.

It's all a mystery and somewhere before my life began it also ended, to begin again and unravel the many pieces of the puzzle of who I am. The Mantis Man was gone, and I met a new friend, not a critter or animal he was my "Robert" that very first day of kindergarten, it was like he had waited for me, for so long. It was as if he knew the Mantis Man had to go. He would be my new friend, a friend that would appear throughout the years, seemingly in very unsuspecting ways. Who would have thought, even in my wildest imagination he would come to me again as an adult after all those years! The connection was still so strong, I would be reunited with my first love!!!

"My Robert!

KINDERGARTEN

I started kindergarten in the fall that year. I was in Miss Selvey's kindergarten class when I first met him. He was made of sawdust, his hair and face as well were all painted on. He was very old, but as a child I didn't know that and I certainly didn't care. His eyes were captivating and his smile was contagious. I knew the moment he looked at me from the bottom shelf in the back of the room that he was my friend.

I remember seeing him laying there on the shelf a forgotten toy, one that no one had played with for a very long time. I picked him up and smiled as his thin drawn lips smiled back at me. His eyes met mine and we seemed to connect like we understood each other. I knew at that moment he was mine!

I would sit with him for hours and tell him my secrets every chance I got. I refused to play with the other kids in the class, I was perfectly happy and content with my Robert. Actually I don't remember if that is a name I made up or perhaps a name he told me. I sometimes called him Robert Charles.

He had somehow mesmerized me and we belonged together. I guess there were to many children in the class, so Miss Selvey didn't notice the strange connection between the two of us. Sometimes at story time Miss Selvey would allow us to hold a toy while she read. I always held my Robert I would never play with anything else. Sometimes he would tell me secrets and make fun of a story she was reading. I would suddenly laugh and whisper back in his ear. She would yell at me and threaten to send me to the corner if I didn't be quiet.

15

I refused to take a nap without my Robert, and when I had to leave for the day I would hug him tightly and kiss him. I would wrap my blanket around him carefully and hide him on the bottom back shelf where he felt the safest. I always whispered I love you Robert Charles I'll see you soon!

He used to get me into a lot of trouble sometimes. Miss Selvey would be teaching us something, Robert would make me laugh. Sometimes at nap time I would whisper secrets to Robert and keep the other kids from getting their rest. Miss Selvey would then take Robert away from me and sit him on the shelf. I would protest and promise to be quiet but, she would take him anyway. I would glare at her and look at him from across the room he would make me laugh and she would yell at me again!

Sometimes when her back was turned he would come back over to me and then I would rest. I remember her yelling at me for getting up and getting him again. She would shake her head and say, "You are really sneaky!" Since the shelf was very tall and I was the runt in the class she would say, "I don't know how you did it but, don't do it again!"

He was magical my Robert Charles and he knew things and sometimes he would tell me stories of castles and such. I loved my Robert!

I remember one day in particular, I was playing with my Robert. Just the two of us as usual in the back of the room away from all the others. One of my classmates decided she wanted to play. I wasn't in the mood to share after all no one wanted to play with him before and I wasn't about to let them play now!

She tried to take him away from me so I hit her and pushed her down! She ran away crying and told the teacher on me. What a baby I thought and I still refused to give him up as Miss Selvey intervened.

I was sent to a corner and told not to get out of that chair until I was told. I sat there very angry and glared at the girl from across the room. I watched her as she picked my Robert up and sat down to play. He looked at me and smiled with a knowing kinda look, one that only he and I could understand.

I smiled at him and gave a little snicker like we shared some hidden secret. I remember hearing a faint whisper as I shook my head yes. But I honestly don't remember what was said. All of a sudden she threw him down on the floor and ran away crying! She seemed somehow frightened as she ran over to Miss Selvey sobbing and pointing at Robert!

Robert gave me a mischievous look and I smiled back at him. Miss Selvey looked at me, then at the doll. She thought I had done something to make the girl cry, but I sat just where she put me, and Robert, laid alone on the floor patiently waiting for my return.

Miss Selvey dismissed the incident soon afterward and directed her to other toys and the incident was soon forgotten. No one bothered Robert after that, no one dared take him away again. No one came to my little kindergarten corner where I sat day after day all alone with my Robert!

I don't know really what frightened her so, I was only five and I didn't care. I was just happy she didn't want him anymore. I guess I'm not surprised my teacher didn't seem to connect the relationship between me and Robert. But, then again maybe she did because she would take Robert away and make me play with the other children or toys.

I wasn't having it. When she would take Robert away and make me play. I would just do something bad, hit or kick someone, only to be put back in my little corner near my Robert. Maybe back in the day people chose to ignore the things that didn't make much sense or things that you couldn't explain for fear of being ridiculed or the threat of being locked, up at the mention of such goings on.

I seem to remember her face as being a little puzzled at times but she never made her suspicions aware at least to my knowledge anyway. At recess I would sometimes sneak back into the class room and play with Robert. We would hide behind the shelves so as not to be seen.

I enjoyed his company and I felt safe with my Robert, he was my hero, so brave and he was always smiling at me. He never scolded me and I knew he loved me, only me, and I was his special little Princess he told me so.

When Miss Selvey caught me she took my Robert and put him on a high shelf so I couldn't reach him. I was sad and hung my head in a pouty way and stomped my feet as she made me go outside. I refused to play with the other children, so she made me sit by the building until I could behave. When she wasn't looking I peeked thru the window on my tippy toes. I was very small for my age and the window was so high. I caught a glimpse of him sitting patiently on the shelf, smiling at me. He always made me feel better, I smiled back at him and waved to him as someone grabbed my arm, scolding me as she pulled me away from the window.

Once back in the classroom we were served our usual milk and cookies and put down for our nap. Without my Robert it was hard for me to just lay there and see him on the shelf. It made me sad as a silent tear fell across my cheek. I closed my eyes to wipe away the tear when I felt something touch my cheek. I opened my eyes to see his smiling face looking at me! I hugged him and soon fell asleep.

When nap time was over the lights came back on and the sound of Miss Selvey's voice echoed through the room. It was story time. After we put our mats away we joined her on the story mat. I sat in the back as I usually did away from the other children. She gave me a surprised look when she saw my Robert sitting with me.

Again she said "I don't know how you got that doll from the top shelf, do you want to tell us?" I just smiled and said "I just wished he'd get down and he did, my Robert is magical you know."

I remember the strange look on her face, and she seemed a little nervous as she dropped the book onto the floor and fumbled trying to pick it up. She looked at my Robert then her eyes focused on the book as she started reading. Her voice seemed a little shaky and she didn't look at my Robert or me the rest of the day.

After I was caught sneaking in to play with my Robert I had to think of another way. I started sneaking him outside and as soon as I got out the door I would run as fast as I could across the field to the far end of the fence, a long way from the play ground. The grass didn't get mowed as well since it was so far from the playground so it made a perfect hiding spot for me and my Robert.

I remember one day I was playing with my Robert sitting in the tall weeds. I was so involved in the playing that I didn't hear the teacher's bell to announce recess was over. I don't know how much time had passed, but I had fallen asleep by the fence holding my Robert. I awoke at the sounds of a lot of people yelling out my name.

The weeds were taller than I and the school seemed so far away, I stood up rubbing my eyes as the bright sunlight seemed to blind me, the gentle winds blew the golden rod and the smell of honeysuckle filled my nostrils. I wasn't sure why they were yelling my name and their voices sounded funny not really angry, but almost anxious.

I heard someone call my name from behind me where the fence met the road. I turned to see a smiling familiar face. "What are you doing out here?" he spoke in his usual friendly tone, not at all like the others, yelling my name. I smiled back at him as he reached over the fence to pick me up.

He waved to the others and yelled "She's okay I've got her." He carried me around the fence by the parking lot to the front of the school. He was a gentle man and I loved him almost as much as I loved my Robert.

He never scolded me and he took good care of me. He was the city bus driver. I was to small to walk to school as it was pretty far away from where we lived. My mother would put me on the bus everyday and "Tom" the bus driver would see to it I arrived to school safely. He would bring me a flower from his wife's garden every day. I would sit on the seat closest to him and I would fall asleep holding the flower. Once at school he would gently wake me and help me down the steps.

I remember one particular day I was surprised to see Tom wasn't driving the bus. I climbed up the steps and sat down as far away from the strange man as possible. I soon fell asleep on the long ride and when I woke up the bus had stopped and nobody was on it. I sat up and looked around, I was surprised to find I was downtown!

I recognized the dime store on the corner. I wasn't sure why the man didn't take me to school, so I got off the bus. Everything seemed so tall. People were bustling about almost stepping on me as I bravely walked down the busy street. I was starting to get hungry and I wasn't sure where home was. I remember not being afraid, I was more curious than anything, and I loved going downtown.

Just as I was trying to get across the busy street I saw "Tom" coming down the road! He looked surprised to see me but smiled and knelt down with arms wide open to welcome me as I ran to him. He smiled as he picked me up, "What are you doing downtown?" He said in a jovial way.

"Where is your mommy? He asked as he thought since I was downtown she must be with me. I explained I had fallen asleep and the man didn't take me to school! He seemed shocked then that I was alone downtown, he said "It's almost noon, you must be hungry." I knoded and he took me to the dime store and ordered lunch for me. He then carried me and my lunch to the bus and took me safely to school. This time he went inside with me and explained what had happened. I remember my Robert looking at me from the door waiting for me. I was safe with both of my very favorite guys! My hero's!!!

Here he was again my knight in shining armor carrying me safely to everyone that called my name endlessly. He carried me to the front of the school I was met by Miss Selvey and the principal along with several other teachers and some sixth graders that had all been looking frantically for me.

I think they were mad at me but, were also glad that I had been found. Tom stood me safely on the ground and told me to stay closer to the other children when I was playing so I would be safe. He smiled at Miss Selvey and said "She has a way of getting lost, and she's just a little mischievous, but she's a good little girl.

Miss Selvey looked at me and then at Robert. I could tell she was disappointed. She just shook her head, took me by the hand after thanking Tom and lead me back to class. I had been missing for over two hours as it was almost time to go home. She scolded me and told me to never do that again I swear you and that old doll will be the death of me!

I didn't know what she meant I knew my Robert wouldn't kill her and I certainly wouldn't! I just looked at her in confusion as I hugged my Robert and wrapped him in my blanket kissing him and promising to see him tomorrow.

I did take my Robert back outside and into the field, after all that's where I felt the safest. But I promised Tom I would be a good girl and go inside when it was time.

It was a sad farewell to my Robert as the school year came to an end. I held him close and whispered I would come back as soon as I could. I wrapped him in my blanket and hugged him tight. I kissed his face as I carefully hid him on the back shelf. I laid him way at the bottom so no one would bother him. I waved goodbye on the sidewalk as I walked hand in hand with my papaw as we passed the kindergarten room.

The following fall school started once again only this time I wasn't in kindergarten. But I never missed the chance to sneak into Miss Selvey's class to say hello to Robert. He was still just as I left him wrapped safely in my blanket waiting for me.

When my first grade classmates went out to play I snuck in to talk to Robert. On occasion I would sneak him outside to play in the field, and as I promised I always went in when I was supposed to. This went on until my second grade when I was transferred to another school closer to my home. As all children I finally forgot Robert and went on to other things knowing I would never see him again.

Who knew the strange events that would connect us together again after years apart, but, then again didn't we belong together!

POOR LITTLE DEAD THINGS

We lived in the same school district as I had attended kindergarten, first grade and the beginning of second grade. I guess there were just to many kids so they separated some of the students to another school. It was closer to our home anyway and not so far that I couldn't walk, unlike my long journey on the city bus. Maybe it was because they wanted to separate me from my Robert. Whatever the reason I had no control over it.

It was really kind of strange how the school was set up. The newer school where my "Robert" lived housed kindergarten, thru sixth grade, I guess the way it was set up was the census and so many kids went to where they had an opening. My brothers and sisters went to the old school which was closer to home. That's why I rode the bus all alone. When I think of it I find it a little odd that I was secluded even back then. Heck, maybe I just would never be a part of the family! Now the school switched agendas once again and they now would go to the new school and I alone once again at the old school! Crazy!

I wouldn't get to see Tom the bus driver, my friend as often as I would have liked. Thank goodness for Saturdays as sometimes we would all ride the bus to town with Tom!

I liked our new school it was across the street from the big park that we would often go to. The little neighborhood grocery was on the corner just across the street from the school. My papaw would often wait until it was time or almost time for school to end so he could walk me home. Sometimes the teacher, probably eager to get rid of me would let him take me early and I would go the store with him.

There was a long brick building across from the school. I could see it from my class room, and I would often hear crying, then a little later lots of cars. The building was not really very large and I sometimes wondered how so many people could get in.

I also wondered why so many people always left crying! Was it a doctor's office or was it a place where people went when they were bad and got in trouble like the principal's office!

Some of the older kids would tell us people went there and never came back! I had walked beside the building before and tried to look inside the windows but, they were covered with heavy curtains. Not counting the fact that I was very small as well as short for my age.

I was always curious about everything and one day I got my chance to see just what all the crying was about. My papaw came as usual and the teacher let me go. This time I got to go to the store and papaw bought me some candy! I was his favorite, although I wasn't the youngest I was the runt. I think he loved me most cause I was number four and hardly mattered at all.

When we left the store I could see the doors were open in front of the building. People were starting to gather, most of them were black people and had on dark clothes. My papaw spoke to a man wearing a black suit and a white shirt, the lady with him had a blue hat with a black feather. I liked her hat, her dress was the same color and she was wearing high heels. I guessed this must be a church as everyone was dressed up.

Another man joined the conversation and I was soon forgotten. I had my chance! I snuck into the building, it was a lot larger room than I expected with rows of chairs and a path going down the middle. I remember it was really kind of dark for someone expecting so much company.

I remember it smelling a little funny and I felt somehow different. I got a sudden chill as I ventured toward the long box sitting in front with flowers all around. I was very small for my age and could barely see inside. I jumped up just a little, enough that something caught my eye.

I looked for something to stand on so I could get a better look. I moved one of the flowers over and stepped up. A black woman was just laying there. She was wearing a long black dress with a white lacy collar around her neck, her dark hair had streaks of grey and she laid ever so still.

I remember thinking what a strange bed and why was it in the front room. Couldn't they wait until she got up before they came to visit? It was really quite a peculiar bed with a lid and all.

I backed away just a little because in my mind I thought she was a vampire and would wait until just the right moment and grab me! She had a slight grin on her face and almost didn't look real as I stared at her. I thought she was kind of rude to be laying there asleep in the church. Didn't she know people were just outside.

Then I saw it, she was holding it. It looked very small in her arms. It was all wrinkled and didn't have much hair. It lay as still as she. It too was black and it wore a long black dress with the same white lacy collar. It looked like the little dollies in the dime store downtown. It was just a lot bigger and was wearing clothes instead of just a diaper. They were thirty nine cents each and I remember I wanted one so bad and every time we went to the store I would play with them until my mom was finished shopping.

I didn't know much about money except that mom always said "We didn't have any." I was so happy to find such a prize and wondered if the lady would mind, since she was asleep and all, if I just held the doll, just for a minute.

I knew I was to never touch things that didn't belong to me. But I wanted that little black doll in the dime store so much and this one was so much bigger. I just wanted to hold it and then I would put it back. No one was there, the lady was asleep it would be okay. I wouldn't drop it or nothing, I would put it back before anyone came in. No one would know.

I reached in to pick it up. I just wanted to hold it for a second. I was still a little to short and soon forgot about the vampire lady as I had my eye on the prize! I held on the side of the box and lifted myself forward just as I reached across to pick up the baby, strong arms were around my waist lifting me away!

I was startled at first thinking the vampire had awakened and I was toast, when I felt the warmth of my papaw! He carried me out into the sunlight. I remember how bright it was after being in the dark room. I decided no wonder vampires stay inside, they are so used to the dark it has to hurt their eyes!

I remember when he put me down I looked behind us just to make sure she didn't come for us. He held my hand as we walked past the now large crowd of people. Some were crying and others just looked so sad. I didn't understand, as we walked home I asked my papaw if maybe Santa could get me a doll like the one the sleeping lady had.

He told me it was one of a kind and it was on its way to heaven with its mommy. We never discussed the incident after that. I had never seen dead people before, nor understood the why's of it. I guess another chapter in my life's journey toward my destiny was continuing to form.

Even after I knew it was a funeral home and I touched the bodies of those that would never breathe again I wasn't afraid. What a strange child I was!

Oh, by the way I got that dime store dolly soon after that! I guess they decided children shouldn't play with dead things!

THE TEENAGER

It was an exciting day for us we were moving across the river into a very big and beautiful old house. We had never had an upstairs before and I just couldn't wait. The rooms were so big and there was finally enough room that we could share bedrooms in pairs of two! There were six of us kids, my mom and dad and my grandpa living together. Mom and dad's room would be downstairs and my grandpa's room also downstairs across from the bathroom. It was just prefect.

My dad worked the late night shift so most of the heavy stuff would have to be moved when he came home at midnight. Before he went to work the sofa was moved. Probably the most important because it had a pull out bed and that meant they would be putting us kids to bed. The remainder of things would be moved well after midnight.

The house was kinda spooky at night, I remember the empty rooms and the echoes we had experienced earlier in the day, yelling back and forth at each other as we explored each and every room.

Now with the night creeping in, the house seemed scary in some ways. It was as if all sound had stopped, it was just to quiet.

Just outside the third upstairs bedroom which, because there was a small balcony, one can only assume it was the master bedroom. There was a room all by itself. It was not really in the house but yet, still a part of the house. The door unlike all the others was locked as if to say keep out.

There were not only six kids, but six very curious kids and how dare they give us such a find and tell us to stay out! We wiggled the lock, we searched for a key, we pushed then pulled, my brothers kicked it and still it would not open. That didn't stop us though. We refused to give up, after all there could be toys inside or even, we imagined treasures to die for! Heck, maybe even a skeleton or two. The more things we came up with, the more excited we became!

We finally got good old papaw that's what we called my grandpa. He was always my hero! He could fix anything! It didn't take him long as he handed a key to my sister. He told us it was a skeleton key and it would surely open any door. A skeleton key! Wow! Were we ever excited! We were more convinced than ever that we would find a treasure or at least some old bones of a pirate or something!

We all stood outside the door on the little balcony, our eyes glistened at the prospect of what was inside. One would think it was Christmas as our excitement grew. The key was finally inserted into the lock, the knob was turned and slowly the door was opened!

I remember the boys were disappointed as the room revealed several old mirrors, and a few books along with a cloud of dust and that awful musty odor! We didn't understand why the mirrors were locked away. You could tell they were very old and the black was starting to appear on the reflective side and it to was very murky and dusty like they had been there for many years.

We girls were a little more excited and recalled some spooky stories about old mirrors. We decided that the mirrors had captured evil entities and trapped them there forever. If we were to look into the mirrors we would surely see them. But if they were waiting, and they saw us first, they would escape and take over our bodies, forcing us to be them! Who knew that I would apply a technique called scrying and look into the souls that may or may not be trapped inside years later. I guess my destiny was forming long before I could possibly know. With that note my sister once again locked the door, making sure what ever had been trapped stayed inside!

The staircase was all wooden which echoed our footsteps even louder. I can imagine what it was like for my parents as six kids ran up and down the stairs ump-teen million times a day. It would be certainly almost impossible for us to sneak down without being heard.

The car lights cast an eerie glow that spread from the front wall all the way into the dining room. We laid there for awhile making shadows as each car passed. Laughing and making faces at each other. It reminded us we were not entirely alone in this new house. Although all the grown ups had left some time ago to get the rest of our belongings I felt safe.

The window seat wrapped around the entire living room right below the large windows that looked out onto the fairly busy road. We had hidden beneath the seats earlier that day to play hide-n-seek. The house had so much character and ambience, oh, how I loved that old house.

We entertained ourselves as we were just to excited to sleep. We would pretend there were vampires hiding beneath the window seats. Their make believe coffins no doubt. We were kids with imaginations and what one didn't think of, the other one did. Someone would sneak over and lift the lid just enough to make the creaking sound of it opening. Then scaring their self as well as the rest of us, would drop the lid causing a big bang! That alone with the echoing of the large vacant house, was enough to scare the bejevies out of anyone! They would run as fast as they could back to the safety our sofa bed. We would scream with delight then cover our heads and peek out just enough to see if Dracula would make his appearance!

We waited to see if Dracula would open the coffin and suck the blood from our bodies! Then, one of us would start tickling the other one and start all of us laughing and tickling each other. With the insistence of my dad we finally settled down after the first batch of furniture arrived. We would be starting a new school the next day. I would be in the second grade.

My parents once again left, it was the wee hours of the morning. I laid there wide awake just to much excitement to sleep. My younger brother and sister were asleep on the sofa bed beside me, while my two older sisters and brother slept beside us on the floor. The staircase was across the room from where we slept and the bathroom light was on at the back corner of the large open room. Its light cast just enough light that we could see if we needed to get up for anything.

I heard a noise from across the room I turned over thinking one of my siblings may be awake. I heard someone say "I'm over here". I looked up and standing there at the bottom of the staircase was this teenager. I knew he shouldn't be there and I didn't hear him come down the stairs. I was a little confused that the echoing of the house seemed to stop. His presence had been undetected.

He stood leaning against the stairway railing, smiling at me. He wore a green corduroy jacket, a white button down shirt. It's collar lying over the collar of the jacket. He wore a green cap that reminded me of one that kids wore back in the thirties, yet are still seen today. It was like a beret but had a bill on it and laid kinda flat on his head. He was smoking a cigarette, blowing rings of smoke into the air. I was always fascinated with how people could make the rings of smoke so perfectly and obediently. I watched as the rings of smoke went higher into the air and then vanished with no trace they had been there at all.

I was fascinated with him, he had a kind face and a shy smile his eyes were friendly as he looked at me. I knew I should somehow be afraid, after all he was a stranger that made no noise when he entered. He was smoking and he was a kid, and he should be at his own home in his own bed! Why was he here?

It was as though he could read my thoughts. He flicked his cigarette and smashed it on the floor, I think he knew I would not tell on him. He pulled another cigarette from his pocket. When he struck his match and raised it to his face, he spoke again.

As he held the match to light his cigarette his eyes grew a little darker, but still I wasn't afraid. However, I was very confused at the words he spoke to me. Actually it was more of a command but his voice was matter of fact and very calm.

He said "kill her". I guess without him telling me who to kill I must have understood who he was instructing me to kill. I remembered looking at her, then back at him. Again he spoke, "kill her". I was confused, why would I do that?! I looked over at her again, this time she wore beads of gold and a tiara on her head, she looked like a sleeping princess. I looked back at him and shook my head no. After all she was my baby sister.

Again he said in the same serene voice as he flicked ashes onto the floor, "kill her now". "you know you want to". I looked at her again, my young mind couldn't comprehend doing such a thing. She donned the beads and tiara on her head and she slept so peacefully. We didn't have any of those things, I was confused as to where they came from as well as how she was able to get them while see slepted I turned to him again. This time he wasn't leaning on the banister he was standing with one foot on the bottom stairs. He made his final demand, in a harsh menacing tone. His eyes became darker than anything I could remember, he glared at me. "kill her, kill her now!" and then he was gone.

I saw him go up the staircase, no noise did he make, I waited to hear the echo that rang so loudly just hours before. There was just silence, no doors opened, no more smell of his cigarette. When I looked at my sister again the beads were gone and she wore no tiara on her head!

A loud bang from over our heads startled my older siblings. I pointed to the stairs told them someone was upstairs. Another bang could be heard and jolted them to their feet. My brother grabbed his baseball bat as they ran to the stairs, I ran closely behind them! The echoes that were so familiar rang out like a stampede of horses, as the four of us jetted up the stairs!

When we got to the top of the stairs no one was there. We looked in every room no sign of anyone. We went back to bed. I never spoke of what the teenager told me to do, and to this day I don't know why I didn't tell.

The next morning I was surprised to find the door on the mirror room was open. Although just a little crack I remembered it had been locked just after we discovered the treasures. I snuck over very quietly to peep in, I just knew he was there hiding, waiting for me. When I finally opened the door the mirror caught my reflection. Other than myself trapped for that brief moment the room was empty.

I never saw the teenager again, but I often wondered if he was the culprit behind my reign of terror that I in flicked on others the following year. After all, didn't he tell me to "kill her"!

THE MAN IN THE CLOSET

We lived in the old house for less than a year. I was sad to find that we had to move as they were going to tear the house down. The structure of the house was as sturdy as the day it was built. I heard my papaw say it many times. It seemed a shame they would be making a motel right beside it and that's the reason it would fall.

Funny thing was after they tore it down and built the motel it wasn't even on the same ground as the house stood! I shake my head every time I pass by the old place. What a waste to such a nice house.

I also think of the teenager and wonder where he went. Now as an adult, I wonder if he haunts the motel as he did our home so many years ago. As a child I never once thought he was anything but a real live boy.

On the other hand, maybe I did. Maybe I've always known. It's like a bond between this world and ours. It seems to have some kind of hold over me, some kind of quest. Some kind of strange trust a bond greater than I can fully understand. I thirst for the knowledge of that doorway to the unknown. I guess that's why I am what I am to this day. Each encounter making me more and more aware. Pulling me in, yearning for the truth. Yet, still giving me a shield so I am not afraid, still keeping me from the whole truth but giving me enough to pursue.

At what point does a child tell? I was that child, and I still can't answer my own question! I didn't talk about anything to my family about the things I seen or heard. Maybe even as a child I was afraid they would make fun of me, taunt me, tease me or worse yet, have me committed!

I remember when we moved into our new house. It was winter and the snow covered the ground. It was almost Christmas and I missed our old house. I imagined how beautiful the tree would have been in the large room.

The living room was small in the new house. The tree sat in the corner of the room. When the sofa bed was pulled out for the night, it's branches touched the bottom of the sleeper. Although the tree was beautiful it looked out of place in the small room.

I wondered if perhaps the teenager had ever visited my dad. He seemed to change after we moved. I thought maybe he loved the old house as much as I did and maybe missed it the same as I.

He started drinking heavy especially on weekends. My parents seemed to fight more after we moved in. He even tried to kill us by setting the tree on fire. It became a ritual. I started liking him less, I never forgave him for the things he did but there were times when he was nice. I wondered if the teenager told him to "kill" us because I didn't do as he told me to do. Maybe it was after all my fault.

I remember on Wednesday nights it was lucky buck at the drive in theatre. My mom always had to work so he would take us especially if there were scary shows on. Often he would drive through the cemetery on our way home. He would go real slow and then jerk the car a few times then shut it off.

He would tell me to get out of the car I was the smallest and fastest and I should go for help. Funny how the car always seemed to breakdown by the really old tall stones that looked like zombies in the darkened night!

I would protest but he would make me get out anyway. My older sister would tell him to leave me alone but it would do no good. So, I would make the sacrifice. I slowly got out and he would wait until I started to run then tell me to go slowly until I got closer to the fence.

That was so they didn't notice me until I was almost out. He would wait until I got a little ways away then start the car and take off! I would run after the car, he would stop, when I was almost to it he would drive away!

Finally I would just stand there watching the car as it drove further away. Once he left me standing for what seemed like an eternity. I remember it was starting to rain and it was getting foggy. The stones seemed to take on their own shapes and I thought I saw something moving in the shadows. A cold chill seemed to come from my feet and travel up my body. I knew I wasn't really alone, yet, I didn't feel threatened even under the circumstances. Probably why I'm so weird today!

I knew it was just another one of his sick games and he wanted to make me cry. I don't remember being afraid, perhaps I was just to angry at him. I knew I wouldn't cry, I vowed that when he tormented my cat.

Sometimes the way we react has everything to do with what happens next. I stood there the stones seemed to move toward me! Shadows darted in and out, as if playing some kind of hide-n-seek.

I heard footsteps coming closer to me, strange noises seemed to surround me! I searched the darkness. I was surrounded with virtually nowhere to hide! The car nowhere to be seen. I ran behind a large tree and sat down, trying to see thru the mist. Waiting, all the while trying to figure out where the gate was. I knew my mom would make him come back for me. I decided I wouldn't make it easy for him I would stay hidden.

If I was quiet enough maybe those that played wouldn't notice me. Maybe I would teach him a lesson! He would have to get out of the car into the darkness with them to find me! I smiled a little at the thought of him out here alone as I, with them!

Then I thought he never left me this long before, maybe something already got them! Coldness engulfed my entire being. The fog was growing thicker and I was the coldest I had ever been, I knew it wasn't just from the rain, but something else. A flash of lighting lit up the stones, I could see many faces looking at me Maybe it was the ones that took my family!

Suddenly there the car was now at a standstill I could see the tail lights. No one got out of the car, he yelled for me, waiting for me to come running like a scared rabbit. I just stood there in front of the tree. I knew he couldn't see me. Something came over me, I didn't really care. He left me, it wasn't the first time. I knew he never wanted me in the first place.

I felt warmness radiant thru my body, all of a sudden I didn't want to go with him. I could hear my brothers and sisters yelling at me to come out! They seemed to be afraid, I could hear it in their voices. I stepped into the pathway. I stood there starring at the car. I was different now, he would never break me!

It was like the battle of whose castle would crumble first, I decided it would not be mine! However it started to rain a little harder, a loud burst of thunder sent me running toward the car. The car door opened I stopped and stared at him, I imagined with eyes I had seen many times from him. Cold, dark and empty! I didn't say a word, my eyes spoke for me. He looked at me, and laughed and asked me why I hid!

I didn't talk much or if at all to my dad after that. He became ever so cruel. I remember one day my mother was sick and he told me she was dying, he told me she had leukemia and she was throwing up blood. I was devastated and heartbroken.

I couldn't understand why he wouldn't take her to the hospital. As It turned out she had a flu bug and was all better after that. He told me my oldest brother had polio and would soon die. I don't know what I would have done if it had not been for the man in the closet.

The closet was one of those back in the day that was built high off the floor. I don't know the reason for it, but I guess they had one as many homes were built with the same concept. I remember it being so high I had to put my hands on the floor of the closet and jump up.

It was my special place. I would go there and hide when they fought or when I was in trouble. Which was a lot it seemed after we moved. That's when I met the man in the closet.

He was a very tall man probably around late thirties or early forties. He always wore the same white button up long sleeve shirt and a pair of dark pants. He seemed to know when I was in trouble and would be waiting for me. He would grab my hand and pull me up into the closet with him.

He would listen as I whispered my secrets to him and tell of my problems. He would always make me laugh and feel better no matter what I had done, he never got mad at me! He had a kind face and even when he smiled I could sense a sort of sadness about him. When I was sad or scared he would put his arms around me and assured me it would be okay.

I went thru a reign of terror when I reached the age of nine. I was very mean at school and in- flicked pain on anyone that looked at me wrong.

I remember I was on the playground minding my own business when a group of my classmates, boys, that is surrounded me in a circle. They started teasing me and taunting me trying to get me into trouble. I tried to get out of the circle but they came closer each time I tried to escape.

Finally I had had enough! I warned them I was going to hurt them! But they just laughed. Which really made me mad! I closed my eyes and started spinning around faster and faster. I clenched my fists and like a whirlwind I hit each of them really hard in the jaw as I spun out of control!

The circle was broken as I heard their cries over the laughter that filled the playground. I ran free, but with one of the bigger boys gaining on me. I ran to the teeter-totters and ran up one side and stood bracing myself for the "kill". As he came closer to me, I waited, until just the exact moment. I had one chance I knew I had him! I jumped on the other end and skinned him from head to toe with the end of the teeter-totter!

Meanwhile the others ran for the teacher as a bloody boy fell to the ground crying. You guessed it I got my ass whipped with the old paddle that hung in the principal's office. Back then they needed no permission to make kids aware of consequences of their actions.

I had several fights that year and several paddling's, but it didn't seem to stop me. After all maybe I was on a mission! I meant to hurt them! Didn't I?

When I got home I ran for my friend in the safest place I knew. He was there just as he promised he would always be. He bent down and held out his hand as he helped me into my haven.

I told him about my day, he hugged me, laughed and assured me they would think twice before bothering me again! He assured me I did only what I could to protect myself.

To make amends for being such a naughty girl he told me where I would find a small box of chocolates on the top of the wardrobe. They looked familiar, I had seen then before a few years ago. I decided I would give the boys each a piece of it tomorrow at school.

So when recess came around I interrupted a game of marvels. They wouldn't let me play cause I was better at it than most of the boys. After all I had brothers and they taught me to play. So I reached into my pockets and pulled out the candy giving each of them a small piece.

They gobbled it down as a devilish little smirk came across my face. I waited a few minutes. One after the other started running for the bathroom. I started humming as I innocently went to the swings and started swinging.

When recess was over the boys were sent home with diarrhea and stomach pains, I ended up in the office, but not before I buried the wrapper of the candy marked EX-LAX, under the swing.

"Yes, I gave them candy, but I don't know why they are sick." I left the office smiling, as I recalled feeding the same candy to my younger brother and sister a few years ago. Did I know what would happen? No, well at least when I gave it to my siblings, but as trial and error would have it, Absolutely!!!

Oh, but it wasn't just the kids at school I was vengeful toward everyone. I remember picking up a brick and throwing it behind my back. I knew she was standing there. But I threw it anyway. Sure enough the cries rang out loudly behind me as my little sister held her head. The red blood running through her fingers and staining her dress. My brother yelling I'm telling on you. I ran over to her and tried helping her into the house. As we climbed the steps I accidently tripped her and she fell hitting her head on the corner of the step! Geez! Was I trying to kill her?! I could see the teenagers face mocking me.

I was scolded real good after that and I of course ran to my safe little corner of the closet where I knew he would be to consul me. A few days later and I hit her again! Same brick same place on her head! I tried to tell myself she asked for it. She knew I was tossing bricks and she still came up behind me! None the less I was in trouble once again! And so to the closet I ran to the only one that loved me!

The man in the closet understood me, he never judged me and I never questioned why he stayed there. After all it was our secret and he was my friend, at the time my only friend in the world.

I remember playing tag on the four corners of my sisters bed. My little sister and I would chase each other bouncing up and down as we ran from corner to corner. We had been warned several times about jumping on the bed, but as a kid I could justify it because after all we were running and playing tag. Don't ya know the difference?

This went on for several minutes it was a Saturday morning. Dad and mom were still sleeping and I could hear the cartoons playing in the next room. We continued to chase each other and when she got to the corner of the bed where the window was I took a giant leap and pushed her out the window!

The crash of the broken glass and the screams of my little sister tore thru the silent neighborhood like an air raid! My mom and dad raced into the room to see me staring out the window and the scene below. All I can say is oops! Thank God we weren't at the house with the upstairs!

They ran outside and I ran for safety! He was waiting for me as my heart raced. I looked at him with terrified eyes and said "I killed her!"

He smiled at me and assured me she was just fine. But I sure didn't think I would be when my dad got a hold of me! So I stayed hidden for the biggest part of the day. I would peak out every now and then to see my sister playing and the man in the closet was right. She was just fine! Oh, she had a few small cuts as she went thru the glass, but nothing major. The grass was tall and had somewhat cushioned the impact of the hard ground.

I gave her a warning look in case she remembered what really happened. She told them she didn't know, she just fell out the window.

But, I sure did! I didn't want her dead, I didn't mean to push her so hard!

OR DID I?

When we are young and innocent and something gets in are we still responsible? Honestly, if it had not been for the man in the closet I don't know what would have happened to me that year!

It didn't seem to stop with classmates and siblings and it didn't seem to matter about size. I was a terror to all. I remember coming home from school earlier than the rest of the kids, but don't remember exactly why. Then again if I had to guess it was probably due to being in some kind of trouble or altercation with another classmate.

Anyway whatever the reason I was alone. I hadn't been home long til I heard someone come in the back door. Since no one was due home anytime soon it startled me a little. I peeked around the corner of the doorway to see a rather tall man with his back turned toward the door.

When he turned around I could see he was a black man! In our house! I didn't know what to do, I started to run hoping he hadn't seen me. But it was to late! So I said "Get out!" he came closer to me and I ran. He chased me thru the house growling at me. My heart was racing as each step I ran he followed closely! I ran to the safety of the closet! I knew the man would save me!

When I reached the door, my heart sank, it was closed tightly. I couldn't reach the knob. I was trapped!!! I tried to run out of the room when I ran right into the black man! He was standing there waiting for me. Holding a whiskey bottle, I ran past him, he spilled some of the whiskey as he grabbed my arm! I kicked him and bit his hand! He cursed as he let me go. Where was the man in the closet!? He never let me down before! Did the black man lock him in the closet!? He had to know I wouldn't be tall enough to reach the knob, but no one knew about the man! I never told anyone!

The black man was playing with me now trying to catch me off guard. He turned to leave, I hid behind the curtain as I watched him go out the back door. I ran to lock it behind him!

Just as I reached the kitchen doorway the back door flew open and the black man ran towards me! Arms in the air, whiskey spilling, growling like a big bear! I screamed and ran as fast as I could! I only hoped my screams would alarm the man in the closet and he would save me!

Once again I found myself trapped in the last room of the house. I really don't remember exactly what happened next. When I think back to that terrifying day. Sometimes I see myself standing alone and frightened in the middle of the room. The door slams shut catching him at just the right moment. He falls to the floor, he isn't moving. The blood gushes from his head. The whiskey bottle shatters, the smell of liquor fills the room as it splatters on the wall. All is quiet except the pounding of my heart! I know he's dead!

The next time I remember I am standing at the door waiting for the exact moment. He comes, I slam the door hitting him with such force the door rattles and the floor shakes as he falls in a dead silence on the floor. The whiskey bottle is shattered, the smell of liquor fills the room. The blood gushes from his head. All is quiet, except the pounding of my heart!

His dead lifeless body is laying in the doorway, I will have to crawl over him. Did the man in the closet come to my rescue after all? Or was I so frightened I actually killed someone!

I stood there it seemed like an eternity, I looked at the man lying there. He looked familiar, where he was bleeding his black was coming off! Oh my God! I killed my uncle!!!!!

Uncle Golk came to live with us a short time ago. He had gotten a job at the coal yard. Since I was normally in school when he came home I never saw him covered in coal dust. Now he lay lifeless, at the hands of a wicked child. I heard the door open and I crawled over him. When I saw my mother I ran to her and burst into tears! Wailing, "I killed him! I killed Uncle Golk!" I killed him dead!"

I grabbed her hand and pulled her into the doorway. She was astonished to find his large body in a pool of blood lifeless on the floor! She checked him as I stood there shaking. "He's not dead." She said, "tell me what happened to him."

She took care of him while I explained. Funny he never talked to me after that. Only thing I heard him say was "That's the orneriest, and meanest dam kid I ever saw!" My mom replied, "I warned you never piss her off, never back her into a corner, and for peats sake never scare her! She will hurt you!!

Turns out I wasn't the only one that knew of the man living in the closet. Funny how we never talked about him. My older brother finally confided in me. He said the man used to scare the hell out of him and my younger brother!

He was so kind and loving how can you say such a thing I asked. The man showed a different side of himself to me. Why, maybe because he knew I needed a friend? Perhaps, he was preparing me for other things I would encounter? Maybe I reminded him of his own little girl. Then again maybe I just saw him differently thru eyes of a lonely child. Who really knows? However, I too would have been frightened had I seen him the way he showed himself to my brothers!

Turns out we found out our block was nick-named suicide alley. And, for good reason! Our house sat across the street from two neighborhood houses that were separated only with one house in between. Our house actually formed between the three of them creating a fairly good triangle!!!! We being the tip of it.

The two guys across the street both shot themselves in the head and of course died. I do remember that, as we were playing outside when we heard the gun shot. It was then that neighbors had mentioned the other one shooting himself not long before that. I didn't know about the man in the closet for many years. I was saddened when I learned he had hung himself!

My brothers would see him swinging back and forth to afraid to move and too afraid to speak of it! Even after all these years he still shudders when he mentions it. He was even more surprised to discover my playmate was the hanging man!!!!

SOMETHING IN THE WATER

It was a Saturday morning I was the first one up as usual. I ran to the closet to say hello to my friend. I was very excited that day, our teacher had passed out forms for our parents to sign. I wasn't sure if I would be allowed to go since it was downtown, and I was only nine. Then again I went alone when I was in kindergarten and everything worked out okay, "Didn't it"?

The YWCA was starting a Pony Tail Club, it would be an opportunity for me to meet new kids my age and do crafts and things! I loved making stuff and drawing and painting. We would also get to be creative and tell stories and go on trips.

They also offered swimming! That would be the only drawback, my mom was terrified of the water and would never let us kids go near it! She had witnessed her younger sister being caught up in a whirlpool in the river when she was a kid. Had it not been for some teenagers nearby she would have surly drowned. My mom was terrified and would never go near the river again.

I couldn't wait to tell my friend in the closet! He was there as usual and pulled me up. I started telling him all about the "Pony Tail Club" he smiled at my excitement. He told me he liked the way my face lit up when I was so happy! I asked him to please tell my mom and dad to let me go! I told him how my mom was afraid of the water, and I didn't think she would let me go. I tugged at his arm begging him to make her say "Yes". He gave a tender yank on my pony tail and smiled as he told me he would try!

I could hear my mom rattling the pans in the kitchen. With six kids in the house it was hard to get a word in edge wise. I hugged my friend as I jumped down from the closet. My bare feet on the hard floor seemed to be so loud as I ran into the kitchen.

I wondered how the man was going to talk to my mom, it was after all our secret that he was there. Oh well, I told myself, he never lies to me. I smiled as I thought of the prospect of my mom finally meeting my friend. It would be great, he wouldn't have to stay in the closet anymore!

She stood at the stove as I ran into the room. I could hardly get the words out I was so excited. Please, I begged and gave her my sweetest smile. I promised to do whatever she wanted me to do, take out the trash, dishes, dust anything I just had to go! I even promised I would be better in school and not get into anymore fights.

She smiled and said "Well, you will have to ask your dad". My heart sank. I hated talking to him, and hated it even more to ask him anything. He was so mean to me! I figured he would say no just to be mean! Or, he would say "Yes", then not let me go as soon as I was ready! I would have to ask in a way that he would think I didn't really want to go.

I waited patiently, finally he was up. Actually he was in a rare mood. He seemed, dare I say the word (happy)! This was puzzling, so I gave it my best shot. I was surprised when he agreed to let me go! I couldn't believe it, I smiled and jumped up and down, running around trying to find my shoes.

When it was time for me to go he met me at the door. My little sister stood beside him. What a disappointment when he told me I had to take her with me! He reminded me of all the mean things I had done to her and it was a way I could prove I was sorry.

I sneered, at the idea of having to babysit her. I was supposed to go and have a great time, meet new kids, enter with a clean slate, no one knew me there. I protested, but, when he told me I couldn't go unless I took her, I gave in.

He dropped us off on his way to a union meeting. Leaving me with final instructions, "Take care of your sister, keep her away from the deep end of the pool. Stay where the lifeguard can see you."

Once inside I felt so grown up! I was still very small for my age and had a little trouble getting the attention of the lady at the front desk. I handed her the papers and she led us into a very large room. There were lots of kids laying all over the floor and the instructor was doing roll call.

We started out splitting off into groups, some went swimming while others were separated into crafts, arts and games. We were told we would get to do everything including lunch, snacks exercise and story time. What a great day!

Everything was so much fun, it was our time to go swimming! I remember the smell of the chlorine as we went down the stairs. It was such a big pool! It even had a diving board. I remembered my dad's warning (stay away from the deep end.)

We changed clothes in the locker room and followed the rest of the kids to the pool. The instructor stood waiting for us. She proceeded to tell us some rules and then everyone just jumped in! I held my sisters hand as I walked her to the shallow end. We sat on the edge just kicking our feet and splashing water over our heads. It was very noisy with kids laughing and screaming. We decided to get into the pool.

A couple of girls came over to join us, they were probably eleven or twelve. They kept coaxing us to go out further. I didn't want them to think I was a baby, so I ventured out a little further than my comfort zone. I left my sister by the steps and told her to stay there.

We splashed each other a few times until they got bored and swam off. I turned to go back to where I left my sister.

SHE WAS GONE!!

I started to panic, looking into the water and all around the pool deck. The instructors were talking to each other, I couldn't get their attention. I panicked, I didn't see her anywhere! I heard my name somewhere behind me. I turned to see an older girl with my sister. I was so relieved! They were on the other side of the pool, sitting on the edge.

I got out of the water and came to join them. The girls name was Marion, she had just turned twelve and had been coming to the YWCA for several years. We talked awhile and she asked if she could take my sister out a little further. She said she was a very good swimmer and she would teach us. I so wanted to swim! I thought how great it would be to swim with all the other kids!

I hesitated, the words my dad had spoken were clear, temptation was overwhelming and I caved. We played in the water a little, she told me to hold my breath and put my face into the water. I reluctantly obeyed, then she put her arms under my mid section and told me to move my arms and my feet. We did this for a little while. Then she told me to practice on my own.

I was a little scared but did what she told me. I stretched forward and tried to swim, when without the support of her arms I went under! I kicked and moved my arms I finally came up gasping and coughing, spitting out the water I had just swallowed. When I was finally able to breath, I looked around she was gone. I turned to look at my sister she too was gone again! I got out of the pool and looked around, they were not on the deck. I looked at the pool and there they were! My heart feel to my knees she had swam to the deep end with my sister on her back!

The life guards were laughing and not paying any attention to what was going on. I yelled for them, but they couldn't hear me with all the screaming and laughter that echoed throughout the room. I could barely see my sisters face bobbing up and down in the water. I didn't have a choice I ran around the deck towards my sister. I tried yelling to her letting her know I was on my way. I could see her face now, so tiny, so scared.

I don't know what happened, it happened so quickly. I jumped into the water when I saw my sisters arms break free of Marion. Marion just swam away from her as if she had forgotten she was on her back! I splashed around trying to keep my head above water. I could see my sister going down! I don't know exactly what happened, but all of a sudden I had a hold of her. We both were fighting for our lives our mouths full of water, unable to yell for help! Knowing help would not come, I could hear a voice somewhere saying "kill her"! Then another voice echoed in my head "Stay away from the deep end, take care of your sister!"

I tried but we went under, she was holding on so tight, she was not helping! I didn't realize I was so close to the rope, I could feel her grip leave my neck as I silently floated deeper. Suddenly I felt arms around my stomach, strong arms lifting me to the surface.

Someone was holding me up, bringing me to the surface! I coughed and struggled trying to catch a good breath! The rope was now within reach, I grabbed for it! The chlorine was stinging my eyes and when I could finally see, my sister was already holding the rope! I don't remember at what point I lost her sinking into death, but I was really happy to see her!

I turned to thank the person who pulled us from death. We were alone, just the two of us hanging onto the rope. The laughter and screaming continued as kids swam around, life guards still caught up in their conversation. It was as though we were invisible. No one was near us, no one seemed to notice the danger of our situation! I looked down into the water, no one was there. It seemed unlikely that they would have left us and not made sure we were safely on deck. I shuddered as I looked into the pool that gave us pleasure a few minutes before, yet changed so drastically to what could have been our deaths! My sister was still shaking probably from the trauma as well as the cold. I glanced into the pool looking for the one who saved us. No one was near us, no one under us. Nothing but water, some unseen presence saved us, and I was grateful!

We held on tight to the rope we were not quite out of danger just yet. As I looked at our situation, I realized we were on our own! Whomever or whatever helped us, was now nowhere to be seen. I would have to get us out. I told my sister to hang on to my neck and don't let go! I then still hanging onto the rope slowly pulled us to the edge of the pool.

The water was still deep where we were so we couldn't get out. It was hard to have her hang on me as I tried hanging onto the side of the pool. Marion came over from a chair on the deck, "Want some help, "she asked. I nodded as she leaned down and pulled my sister from the water. I pulled myself out and we laid on the deck exhausted!

When I was finally able to breathe without coughing, I yelled at her "Why did you take her out there!" "Why did you just leave her"? "She could have drowned!!! "Why didn't you help us?"

She said "I'm sorry, I forgot she was on my back." "When I remembered I swam back to get her, but I saw you and the man, so I figured it was okay." "Sorry".

I looked around for the man, no men were there, just women and girls. I knew someone helped us I never saw anyone, she had no reason to lie. I was just thankful my sister was okay! I was thankful for the hands that guided us safely to the rope. I couldn't help but think of the consequences I would have to face if it had not turned out the way it did. Either both of us would be dead, or one of us, and if I were the one that survived I maze as well be dead.

Funny, how I tried killing her and ended up risking my own life to save her! When I was able to stand I took my sister into the locker room to shower and get dressed. I told her she was not to tell anyone, ever, what happened. I asked her if she saw the man that helped us, she nodded (yes). I asked her where he went she just pointed down. I couldn't help but shudder when I thought about it. We surely would have drowned that day without the hands of the unseen presence. I wondered if the man in the closet had saved us. He would not have stayed for others to see, as he was my secret.

One thing was sure, Marion put us in that position! We left the building and we waited for her outside. When she came out I punched her in the gut and pushed her down the stairs! Took my little sisters hand and headed home!

THE ATTACK

Mom and dad as I mentioned before worked nights, leaving us basically on our own. Well, that is until the "peeping tom" came lurking around our neighborhood! It was one of those really dark nights, cold and cloudy. The moon peeking in and out of the clouds. The six of us sat eating bowls of cereal and ice cream, watching television. Yes, television, I'm not the dinosaur you thought I was!

The program captured our attention. My oldest sister sat at the end of the sofa near the window, so it was her that heard the noise first. It began as a slight scratching noise, then another only louder this time, then a slight peck. She walked over to the window, we turned the sound down on the television. Our attention went to her and the pecking at the window. We all grew quiet as we looked to our older sister for guidance.

She wasn't sure what to do, after all she was only a seventh grader herself! She quietly pulled the curtain to the side, looking out into the night. All of a sudden she blurted out a blood curdling scream! I dropped my cereal bowl onto the floor. Then she fell to the floor in a dead faint!

I ran to the window and banged loudly on it, startling the intruder, then I ran out the front door with my older brother right behind me! We started throwing rocks at the perpetrator as we chased him down the street! My younger brother let the dog out and he soon joined the chase! We ran into the darkness, the man desperate to get away, his shadow was large as he ran beneath the street light, then into the darkness. I knew we had made contact with the rocks as he would grab his head or back and legs as he ran. The dog was almost on him when he darted between the houses. We lost him but we were pretty sure he would not be back!

We were out of breath as we looked around trying to find the hiding place. After a little while we headed home. Once in the shadow of the street light we noticed a few blood spots on the street. A big high five was shared with my brothers and myself as we celebrated a victory!

We arrived home to find my sisters awaiting our arrival. My sister was as white as a sheet! He had scared her so badly! We assured her he would never be back! We were to excited to sleep and didn't notice the time. Mom and dad arrived home a short time later, we blurted out our story and beamed over our victory. We told of how we chased him and beat him with rocks. As we spoke we re-enacted our roles each taking credit for the blood that was spilled! Little vamps!

Mom asked us what we would have done if we had indeed caught him. My brothers replied they would have kicked his face in and broke his legs so the police could get him! My younger brother chimed in "I would let the dog eat him!" I simply said "I would have killed him!" I looked into my mother's eyes, I didn't smile, the scary part of it all was knowing I would have! I could still hear the teenager mocking me "Kill".

After that night a friend of my dad's came to take care of us. We liked him a lot. He told us wonderful stories about the "Kook-a-mongo Indians". Of course I don't know if there ever was such a tribe, but nonetheless the stories held our attention for hours on end! He was such a great story teller and often he would act out some of the stories!

He gained my trust, something I didn't often allow, after all the man in the closet was the only one I truly trusted at the time. At any rate he helped us with our home work and fixed our dinner. We loved watching television but we loved his stories even more. Often we would play cowboys and Indians, and he would help us make Indian headdresses out of paper. We learned to hoop and holler and he taught us Indian war dances! Great times!

He would often take us to the park to see the animals. The park was wonderful back in the day. There was a monkey cage, a concession stand and closer to the river was all kinds of animals. In the summer the park was full of people, picnics, fishing, soap box derby and stage shows! Sad that has all faded away. Our children would never be able to experience the days and fun we enjoyed and the best part was it was all free! He would make up stories about each one as we passed their cages, then we would add to the stories run and scream and play on the swings. He would give us piggy back rides and play endlessly with us. We loved him!

One night he just didn't seem to be nice, and he smelt funny. The smell reminded me of the moonshine my dad and our neighbor brewed in the garage. I had never known him to drink before and I didn't understand. He sent us out to find objects he had hidden in the yard, after a short story.

I dug deep into the ground beside the garage. I found a bone of some animal and was so excited to show him! We were supposed to make up a story about our findings to share with the others and add to his story. I was putting my story in my head as I headed for the house.

The house was a little dark and I was surprised he wasn't in the kitchen starting our dinner. I walked thru the house. I could hear what sounded like a muffled cry. I opened the bedroom door to find my older sister fighting with him! I was taken aback, I looked at the situation, at first I thought they were playing. I was surprised to see my other sister leap on him from the other side of the bed. I stood there watching, when I realized what was happening I dropped my bone on the floor and jumped on his back!

He threw me to the floor and my sister bit him. I was back on him in a flash and the two of us continued beating him. My older sister had fainted, which sent me into alarm! I couldn't believe what he was doing, I was angry and I exploded into a rage I didn't know I had as I growled and plowed into him fists flying. By this time my older brother came in and also joined in on the beating! Blood was flying, I wasn't sure where it was coming from, but it made me hit harder and I didn't like what I had become!

We were like an animals, we seemed to possess strength from within that could only be from anger and fear. My sister had stopped fighting, she was afraid of what was happening. She could see the madness in my eyes! It was as if I had turned into something sinister, so evil and dark, I couldn't stop myself I had no control! I was suddenly aware I was the only one beating him, it was like he couldn't fight back, or was afraid to. My sister pulled me off him, I was still swinging and kicking, I caught him square in the eye with my foot, as she and my brother pulled me away.

He was bloody, and he was crying like a baby and he staggered out the door into the night! I chased him throwing rocks and a pop bottle that hit him in the head. My brother tackled me throwing me to the ground. Holding me down as I screamed in anger! I was out for blood! He broke my trust, I wanted to destroy him! My hands and clothes were covered in blood. It was not my blood, nor the blood of my siblings. There was a lot of it, I wanted to kill him!

I ran to the closet to my friend and cried, in his arms as he calmed me. I remember sobbing and telling him I trusted him, I loved him, why did he do this! I tried to kill him! I wanted him dead! I looked at the man in the closet," I will wish him dead, he will be dead to me!"

I never saw nor heard of him again. Who knows maybe he was dead!

THE DEVIL DOLL

We had moved once again. Memories were just that, it was time to go forward. My dad had a friend that was town constable. We called him "Buster ". He and His mother were from New Orleans and had a caging background. His mother was quiet a character and I believe to this day she dealt a little if not a lot into the art of black magic.

I was probably ten or eleven by this time so I didn't really know about such stuff only what we saw at the movies or on television. Anyway, by this time Buster and my dad were becoming really good friends. His mother had came to our house a few times and believe me I had seen many drunk men in my life, but never an old black woman. She was so skinny and wiry! They would laugh so loud and she would be so funny when she would get mad at them for whatever reason. Once she put her hand on my head and mumbled something I didn't understand. Then she just looked at me in a trance like state, I figured it was the alcohol taking over her. Guess I shouldn't have laughed at her.

Buster would always make me laugh! He would kiss my hand and say I was a little lily, lilac princess. Whatever that meant! He would try to be poetic but the truth was he was just drunk!

On Sundays dad and Buster would go over to Buster's house and drink moonshine. I remember him coming home late one night and carrying something that looked like a stuffed toy of some kind. It would be the next evening after we came home from school that we would discover what it was.

I was the first one in the door with my younger siblings following. The older kids went to jr high and high school so they would be later. My little sister would discover it first as she passed thru the dining room, she caught a glimpse of it laying on my brothers bed. She and my brother went in together to take a closer look. They didn't like it so they just left it lay. I went in a few minutes later to see what they were talking about.

It was indeed a stuffed toy, one that I couldn't imagine any little kid wanting to play with. I picked it up. It was dirty and was missing a hand or I should say claw. It had on a black vest with a black tie. Its body was red fur and its face was made of some kind of thick rubber. Its face was a bit hideous, with horns on top its head also made from the thick rubber substance. It was a replica of the devil. Its eyes seemed to penetrate deep into our souls as we stood looking at it! I felt we were not alone at that very moment and I didn't like that feeling.

One thing about me was I was not afraid of much probably due to the cemetery episode. What doesn't kill you makes you stronger, what doesn't scare you to death gives you inner strength. Besides it was my younger siblings and I couldn't let them know how much it bothered me. I laid it back down on the bed, I had a sudden urge to run from the room. My hands felt dirty like I just needed to scrub them real good and hard.

I wanted to run but I couldn't scare the younger ones so I waited until my older siblings came home. They looked at it and I could tell they didn't like it either. But, no one discussed it. So, It just laid there day after day. When my brothers went to bed they would throw it in the closet and put the toy box in front of the door.

In the morning it would be placed back on the bed. We laughing referred to it after a time, as the babysitter. We wouldn't go near it at night. We did finally talk about how its eyes seemed to take on an eerie glow at night. We would usually go in twos after that and take a quick peek in probably to make sure it was still there more than anything else.

We would often hear strange noises and sometimes banging late at night. Scratching sounds would echo from the closet as well as whispers! It would scare the crap out of us! Sometimes footsteps could be heard at first like a soft sound then would get louder as it seemed to come closer. Shadows would run across the dining room as though the room were full of candles an eerie glow cast by nothing!

The shadows were dark and huge, not really a distinct shape. I remember one night in particular, I had to go to the bathroom in the wee hours of the morning. I tried waking my sisters but they wouldn't wake up. I had no choice but to go alone thru the darkened house with only a small light glowing from the kitchen stove.

I hesitated as I stepped from the bedroom door into the living room. I could see the dining room. I waited for any sounds or movement of shadows. All seemed to be clear! I took a deep breath and ran through as fast as I could not once glancing toward the bedroom where the devil doll was kept.

I made it! However the journey back proved to be a different story! Memories of sleep walking filled my head as I stirred up the rats a few years ago! Now fully awake no matter how quiet and careful I was, I awakened something more terrifying!

I tiptoed to the kitchen door peeped into the dining room. Just as I stepped across the threshold, I heard the whispers! Then the footsteps! I glanced toward my brothers room hoping one of them would wake up and help me! The eerie glow started filling the room like fog rolling in. The shadows I expected to see did not come. The thing that appeared was large and had a distinct form, my heart raced up into my chest as I saw the profile of the devil!!!!

The horns coming from the top of his head, the smell, the low growl! The shadow he cast was much larger than the dark shadows we had seen before. I was terrified! I stood there not moving, not breathing, I closed my eyes as it seemed to come closer, then it was gone! I didn't know where it went and I didn't really care at the time!

I took a deep breath and ran as fast as I could thru the dining room, living room and finally the safety of our room. I turned around only after I reached the door way, all was quiet. I jumped back in bed and willed sleep to come and erase the terror I had just been in! I knew I must not tell, who would believe me anyway!

The noises and footsteps as well as the shadows continued, I stopped drinking water before bedtime, as I never wanted to go thru the house alone again. I never saw the profile of the devil again, but as long as that thing was in our house I knew he was near!

I heard my dad and Buster talking one night about the devil doll. I heard my dad say what a hideous toy it was and he wanted Buster to take it back to his house. Buster refused saying momma gave that to your kids she won't take it back! It would upset momma!

There was something in his voice when he spoke of the doll. It was as though he himself was afraid of it! Dad insisted he take it back but Buster refused and left the house. The doll stayed at our house for a little while after that. Then it was gone. I heard my dad tell my mom he had tried to take it back to Momma. He said she acted afraid and made him go. She refused to take it back. He said something is wrong with that thing! I never understood why he bought the thing home in the first place. Not to mention it was so hideous, but it was so dirty as well! Who gives their kids dirty, hideous toys!

Sometimes I even suspected that maybe when he was drinking and they were all together that he to may have had a little dealing with the black arts.

I wondered if he to saw what us kids saw in the wee hours, when he would come home from work. Those horrible glowing eyes! Did he ever see the thing I saw or hear the whispers and growls? The footsteps or scratches, the dark menacing shadows? Maybe that's why he started drinking heavier to hide his own fear and gain courage through the bottom of a whiskey bottle! At that time I wanted a big swig of his whiskey too!

I didn't really know what happened to it at the time, one day it was just gone! One afternoon my mom and I were in the truck with dad. We had gone with him to the doctor's office. It was about twenty miles from our house and a nice little ride. On the way back we heard a strange noise coming from somewhere in the truck.

My dad pulled off the road and told us to get out. Oh boy, he hadn't done that in awhile. At least this time it was in the daytime, my mom was with me, and there was no cemetery around! We got out and sat under a tree while he checked the truck out.

It wasn't long before he was pulling the seat forward and slamming it backward. He did this several times, each time he seemed more aggressive. Finally satisfied, we were told to get back into the truck. I remember it being a nice breezy day not to hot even though the sun was bright. The sweat on his brow was now dripping down his face, but I saw something else that day, I saw fear!

We hadn't gotten very far until the noise was back. It was louder this time and sounded like something scrapping against the seat. My dad turned his head toward me, I could see it in his eyes cold, hard set, trying not to show the fear I had seen a few minutes before. Once again he pulled off the road. Something in his voice warned us as we were instructed again to get out and move far away from the truck.

We followed his instructions as he repeated the process of slamming the seat back and forth. We couldn't figure out what he was trying to achieve. He slammed the seat back and forth cursing as he did so. The sweat now covering not only his brow, but the front of his shirt as well.

When he finally stopped we went over to the truck to see exactly what the heck was going on. Mom seeing the look of desperation on his face asked "what in the world is wrong!" My dad finally pulled the seat forward to reveal the devil doll!

But that wasn't all, I swear to you the thing had grown a claw on the side where he had none before. I could see the terror on my dad's face as the devil doll was placed behind his seat, it was impossible for it to have gotten on the other side of the truck!

It was put back behind his seat once again and slammed several times funny it never even looked as though it had been smashed it was as if it couldn't be destroyed!

By the time we reached home it had scratched its way back behind my seat again. We got out and mom ordered my dad to get rid of it! I wanted to tell them what I had seen, as It was pretty clear it was after me! But I never said a word, maybe it was the fear I saw on his face. I knew it was just something I would have to face alone.

I wondered if Momma had sent this evil to our house and to me, what words did she chant that day she placed her hands on my head! Why is the biggest question! Maybe she saw the evil in me from all the times before. But, I didn't mean to be bad, couldn't she see that?!

He took it back to Busters and Momma's house. They made no bones about it they did not want the thing back! It was clear to everyone the thing was evil. So they decided to take it and bury it which they did, somewhere in back of Busters house. They buried it real deep and to this day I could take you and show you approximately where it was buried. Thank heaven for concrete and progress the final resting place of the devil doll! Or was it?

Not long after the thing was gone I was cleaning our bedroom. A picture of my dad's baby brother hung in our room. He was only a child when he died of blood poisoning and I think my dad blamed himself for his death. He only spoke of him when he was drunk. My Grandmother for whatever reason gave the picture to my dad after all those years! I didn't understand why the picture was hung in our room.

I was dusting the headboard of the bed when the picture fell off the wall hitting me in the head! The double string although yellowed through the years was still strong. A wire had also been added for extra support just in case the string gave out. The nail was still in tack. There was no logical reason for the picture to have fallen!

I remember my dad saying it was a sign, and he said he was worried I would die! Somewhere in my mind I think he thought his brother would take revenge on him for his untimely death. After the doll now the picture,

Havoc continued, dad drank almost every night. The effects of its presence in our house still lingered many years after that. Many bad things happened, some I will never speak of. Violence and rage, anger and cruelty were on the rampage. It seemed the devil had gotten in after all.

My dad tried to kill us on several different occasions. From shooting the shot gun through the house to trying to run over us with his car. He threatened me almost on a daily basis, and when his threats didn't faze me he started again with the mental aspect of his sick games.

My brother by this time was in the marines on his way to Viet Nam. He would scream at me over and over "They will send your brother home in a body bag!", it was almost to much to bare. I wouldn't let him break me!

I remember him bringing home an owl, it was huge someone had captured it. He knew some people at the dog pound and talked them into letting him have it for us kids. On one of his mad drunken binges he took the owl from its cage. He asked us if we liked it. When he reached in to get the owl out, its only defense was to bite him. He grabbed it pulling it out of the cage feathers flying. He began hitting it in the head. He continued beating the owl, the blood started trickling out from its face. We begged and pleaded for him to stop but he seemed to take great pleasure in our horror!

The memory of my beloved cat swept over me. I was bigger now I could fight back! He continued his rage, I grabbed his arm with all I had, screaming "Stop it"! His eyes cold, dead and empty, the same heartless eyes I knew so well, burned into my soul. He threw me to the ground, the owl went limp, the beating stopped. He threw it back into the cage. He walked away as though nothing happened! All we could do was watch as the once beautiful owl took its last breath. I held the tears for later, I would not let him know how much he broke me that day. I prayed to God that night to take my dad away. I just wanted it to all stop!

He fought with his best friends that year as well, I remember three of them came to the door one evening. I was outside when I heard the yelling and arguing. I came around the side of the house to see what was going on. They started to run from the front of the house when I saw my dad come after them with his rifle. He shot at them several times, I ran to the side of the house and watched as they made their escape. I knew my dad really didn't want to kill them as he was a better shot than that. He wanted to show them that he meant business, and that he would kill them if he had to. What was happening to him I guess wasn't really his fault. Something evil had just taken over.

A few days later it was as though nothing had happened and they were friends again. That is all but Buster. He didn't come around after the burying of the devil doll.

Once my sister held a shotgun to my dad's head, had it not been for my mom she may have taken his life. Had I been home God forgive me I would have helped her pull the trigger! Ironically the man I had wished dead so many times. I saved his life that year. I guess I wasn't as evil as I thought after all. I still had human feelings even though there were times I felt nothing at all. I often wondered if the devil doll had somehow escaped and was waiting for just the right moment

After all the devil is in all of us in one form or another. We all are greedy at times. We lie, cheat, steal, lust, we hate, we kill, we curse, we have evil thoughts. We gossip and spread rumors, we hurt innocent people in one way or another sometimes without meaning to. Some bargain with the devil and sometimes we turn our backs on God and salvation. Its easier to be bad than good and easier to blame God when things go wrong. Oh I don't mean we do all those things but all of us are guilty of some of the things. Those without fault are the biggest liars!

But when we are devastated we know where to turn and God is always waiting and welcoming us. In my darkest hours of all those things we had no choice to endure. I trusted God would get me thru, he hasn't failed me yet and I know in my heart he never will.

Under all that concrete the devil doll was buried, we never saw it again, but the devil is still all around us and in some of us. Some are just to weak to break free of it. Unfortunately my dad suffered at the will of all evil.

THE MOTH MAN OF WEST VIRGINIA

I remember as a kid we would often go to West Virginia to visit my grandmother. Dad would get home at midnight and we would travel during the wee hours to avoid traffic. I suspect it was mostly so us kids would sleep and he wouldn't have to listen to us! Whatever the case it was a ritual and that's the way it was.

I was about nine or ten we were traveling the winding road headed toward Point Pleasant. We had a nine passenger station wagon and my younger sister and I always sat in the back so we could see where we had already been! Or where the others were first, I always liked being last not realizing it was yet, another link into my destiny that was forming.

It was the wee hours of the morning and I couldn't sleep. I loved looking out into the night at the moon and the stars. They were so beautiful, this particular night however there was something different in the sky.

I could see it from a distance like it was following us. It was rather large as I remembered it from being so far from us. It seemed to enjoy swooping in and out of the tree lines. The closer it got the larger it became. I was mesmerized as I watched it fly, so large yet so graceful. Its wings were huge as he came closer to us I could see just how enormous the wing span really was as it covered both sides of the two lane road.

I could hear the flapping of his gigantic wings as he swooped around the curving road. I must have watched him for a long time it was as though he wanted me to enjoy his journey. I wasn't afraid, it was as if I was somehow caught up in a trance as I watched his every move. Maybe it was the safety of the car that I felt no fear. As he glided down to the back of the car I could see him clearly! It was as if he wanted to peep in or at least see who watched as he put on his show.

I thought it was the biggest bat I had ever seen in my life! Bat's and I seem to have a strange connection through my life as I have had many encounters with them. But, he was definitely the most enormous and those large glowing red eyes! It was like he took a peep into my soul!

I yelled "Mom look at the big bat with the big red eyes!" I suddenly wanted to share him with the others in the car. I knew they would probably never witness anything so miraculous as this! Frankly I couldn't believe they never heard the loud flapping of his wings.

The response was "Your dreaming, go back to sleep." I turned back to watch him as he swooped across the night sky back into the thickness of the tree lines. It was as if he didn't want the others to see, then one last swoop across the road as he seemed to bid me farewell. I never spoke of him again it was like we had some kind of understanding.

I remember it was summer when I saw him and a few years later, so I made no connection to him when my dad had made a trip to West Virginia in December that year. He had just crossed over the silver bridge that we had many times crossed. Before he was all the way home we heard the news of its collapse!

It was December 1967, when the bridge collapsed with no warning. The silver bridge that we had traveled on many times, now gone! The cables breaking away causing a dominoes effect! The mighty bridge swaying back and forth throwing cars and trucks into the cold, deep, dark water below! The concrete that was the road now giving way! Breaking apart as the cables shook them to pieces! Falling and crumbling as it splashed into the night! Christmas presents floated on top of the water and lights from the fallen vehicles shown eerily from the river below! Forty six lives were lost that cold snowy December night.

We being children, were spared the terrible details, and certainly of the tragedy of the lost lives that wouldn't be home for Christmas. It wasn't until many years later that I would learn the "The Moth man of West Virginia" was my enormous bat with the big red glowing eyes! Little did I know then that he would have been seen many times by many people right before the tragedy struck!

Some say creatures such as the Moth Man have been reported making their presence known around the world. Ironically just before a tragedy strikes! It was purely by accident that I heard what I already knew years ago, he was real! I was cleaning house and had the television on. I wasn't paying a lot of attention as I cleaned, but a documentary was announced about the "Moth man of West Virginia."

I'm like what? So I take a break and sit down. It was true events that happened concerning the Moth man creature and the collapse of the silver bridge!

As I listened I was astonished! It was my bat with the large red glowing eyes others had seen him also! But I still didn't understand why they were so afraid of him. I was enchanted! I guess another weird fact has surfaced in the journey of my destiny. Maybe he didn't want me to be afraid!

I grabbed the phone to call my sister in Florida. I just had to know if she remembered that trip. I didn't tell her about the documentary and only asked "Did she remember the night I had a "dream." She finished before I said anything else. "Oh, the bat with the big red eyes!" "You made such as fuss how could I forget."

She was as astonished to learn it was real as I was. I later called my mom and other siblings to see if they too remembered. They also did but none of them saw him or heard the loud flapping of his wings.

I was just glad to finally know what I saw was real, I never would have connected him or blamed him for the bridge collapsing.

I was sorry all those people died and remembered how lucky my dad was to have been almost home when the tragedy struck. I guess we were all lucky as we were supposed to all go to West Virginia, but we had school, and with Christmas vacation a few days away he decided to go without us. Who knows maybe we would have been on that bridge if we had gone!

According to the documentary the silver bridge fell into the cold dark icy waters on December 15, 1967. A strange creature had been spotted in the area by several residents as early as a few years prior as I also had witnessed. Some were so frightened by it they refused to comment. Some say the collapse of the bridge was because of him. No one had seemed to see him after the bridge accident. However sightings of him or creatures like him were spotted throughout the world each time right before tragedy struck. Some said he was very tall and looked like a moth they named him the "Mothman of West Virginia. I knew he was very large and those red glowing eyes I will always remember. Regardless of what they say I think of him as a warning not a disaster. I saw into his eyes and I wasn't afraid. However I was always and still am scared of bridges! Maybe it was a warning somehow making me leery of bridges and the waters below! Maybe he was trying to warn of disasters a guardian angel! Others also stated his horrible red eyes were so frightening. Funny I was intrigued, and very fascinated!

After that I recall our trips were not over the silver bridge, but on a ferry, not far from where the bridge once stood. I would think of all those people that didn't make it home that night. I would look up at the sky perhaps to catch a glimpse once more of the "big bat with the large red glowing eyes!"

HYPNOTIC SUGGESTION

It was spring break, my sister had invited my little sister and I to stay with her and her family for the week. We were excited at the prospect of leaving state and going to Ohio! My niece was just a baby and it would be fun, helping out and spoiling her!

We arrived around noon, unpacked and settled in. It was a small apartment, and my sister had made up a bed in the nursery for us. I promised to take care of my niece, so my sister could finally get some sleep!

She instructed me on where to find things, her favorite toys and how to check her bottle. I was no stranger to changing diapers and I loved kids, it would be a breeze! We ate lunch and went for a drive.

The next day we went to the beach. It was a blast! Although after the scare we experienced at the YWCA when we were younger, neither of us learned to swim.

My brother-in-law tells me to get on his back, I was skeptical but I trusted him. After all he was my brother-in-law, he was strong and could swim like a fish! Besides he promised he wouldn't take me out to far and he wouldn't go under.

Well he didn't tell the truth, he swam further out than promised but I remained on top. He told me to let go and he would teach me to swim. NO and OH NO, that wasn't going to happen! Been there done that! Besides why would the water have to be so deep for him to teach me! I wouldn't budge, hanging on tighter now at the prospect he would unclasp my arms and leave me! He laughed and started swimming closer in to shore. Without warning he went under! Then back up as I coughed and spit water, trying to catch my breath! Then under again, and up, I could hardly catch my breath in between dives!

Thoughts of the YWCA rushed back into my head. What's with adults, and water! The Y they clearly weren't paying attention. He on the other hand, was doing it on purpose!

I caught a glimpse of my sister waving at him to come in, she didn't look happy! Under again, back up! Coughing and struggling for air we finally made it to shore! After I caught my breath I picked up a hand full of sand and smashed it into his face! Thoughts filled my head on the drive home. My sister was very angry at him, the ride back was quiet.

To make amends he stopped and treated us to burgers, fries and a shake! He told me he wouldn't have let me drown. I just replied, "You tried!"

The week was going fast, so the last night my sister took us shopping. A baby sitter was lined up when we got home, by my brother-in-law. He announced dinner and a movie for his three favorite girls! No doubt still trying to make amends for the lake. When we got back home, the baby was already asleep.

We sat in the living room watching television. Some kind of magic show was on, followed by a hypnotic act. We engaged in a lengthy conversation about people being hypnotized. I had always heard if a person wasn't willing, even in their subconscious mind, it would be a failed attempt.

That's when he spoke up and said, "I know how to hypnotize people." It was just a simple statement, "I've read books and studied it." He had this eager look on his face. One that you could associate "Like a kid in a candy shop!" My sister dropped a cup, breaking it to bits as it fell onto the tiled floor. She quickly started picking up the pieces and scurried into the kitchen.

After questions and careful consideration, my younger sister agreed to let him try. I was skeptical, she was willing. It would be interesting to see the results. They seemed to be gone for awhile. I didn't know how long it would actually take, so I waited. After a while longer they entered the room, he was leading the way. She stopped at the doorway, he continued into the room.

He instructed us to yell and clap when she enters all the way in. he told us she thinks she is a singer, none other than "ELVIS PRESLEY"! I rolled my eyes, but yelled and clapped just to play along. She rushed into the room and started strumming her invisible guitar. She bellowed out some verses and started shaking her hips! It was quite hilarious, she came closer to me and started pulling her fake scarf from around her neck. She seemed to wrap it around my neck and in her mind I guess, pull me to the stage.

It's very important he told us that we put ourselves in their frame of mind. I played along, for awhile. Sorry but I just couldn't take it anymore! I after all thought they were playing me. I did think it odd, that my older sister had a strange look on her face the entire time.

She stopped singing, dropped her arms to her side, imaginary guitar I assume hit the floor. She stormed "off stage", out of the room! He quickly followed her. I really hadn't noticed her eyes being so glassy until she stood there staring into my face, before dropping her "guitar".

What a way to bring the curtain down! I felt a little bad that I had laughed at her performance. It was just so funny, and she sounded just awful! Way to butcher an image and a song all at one time! I would never think of Elvis in the same way again!

They were in there for a lot longer than I thought they should have been. I thought to myself, maybe he really did hypnotize her. Her eyes were glassy, normally she wouldn't be able to keep a straight face.

Heck, she in reality, now that I think about it probably didn't even know the words to the song!

We sat and waited patiently. Finally they came out. She looked normal, smiled and asked what happened. I started telling her, she looked at me like I was nuts. He told her she wouldn't remember doing anything. After confirming what I had said by my big sister, we all had a good laugh. Ending with, "you will never make it as a singer"!

"It's your turn." They all teased, looking at me. "Naw, I'll pass." I said.

He said, "Well how are you going to prove your point, if you don't let me try."

"Yeah, since you don't want to be hypnotized, it would certainly validate your take on it."

"Oh, okay, but I don't really want to."

We entered the bedroom. I laid down on the bed. The lights were dim, I snickered. He pulled a necklace from the jewelry box. He began by telling me to relax.

He held the necklace in front of my face, moving it back and forth talking slowly. I couldn't help but laugh at his attempt. His eyes seemed to darken, and his voice getting deeper. I laughed as he was trying so hard to be mysterious. At one point I recognized his eyes, dark, void of emotion. He reminded me of the way my dad looked so many times. I decided it was just the lighting, and wasn't he after all supposed to be "Mysterious!"

I felt like I was being watched it made me a bit uneasy, so I snickered, and pretended to cough. I told him I needed water. He seemed a little pissed that I kept interrupting the session. The door opened about that time and my sister poked her head inside. We must have been in the room far longer than my sister, as she asked "You guys okay?" "I thought you forgot us".

I laughed as he put the necklace back inside the box. We came out of the bedroom. My little sister said "Well, is she going to do anything?" Asking my brother-in-law. "No, she was right it didn't work."

The rest of the night was spent watching television and eating yet more popcorn. We would leave early tomorrow for home. I had crazy dreams that night, but attributed it to late night popcorn and of course M&M's, peanut M&M's! Yummy!

Little did I know then what significance the hypnotic experience would have and did have. Leaving its scar on us, revealing a dark side of someone we all trusted. It would be a few years when I would discover what had actually happened to my sister's. Something dark was indeed awakening.

THE STRANGER AMONG US

By the time I was seventeen, I had had enough! My older sisters had married to get away from home. My older brother joined the Marines. My younger brother spent a lot of time at his friend's house and my sister and I were abandoned by life.

We had managed to survive all the traditional Christmas's of the trying to burn down the tree, which started when I was very young. The gun shots that became pictures embedded not only in the walls of our home, but embedded in our memories as long as we shall live.

The animal cruelty, the drunken fights, the cursing and badgering. The bullying, the threats to kill us that sometimes were way to close. The fighting with us kids to get a fight from my mom, then a fight with my mom to get a fight with us kids. He was never happy.

The grave yard incidents, alone would have unbalanced most children. The devil doll incident, would have sent a grown man over the edge! All in all it's a wonder any of us survived! Angels were near and only God knows what else we endured. For some things are to horrible to speak out loud!

I remember all to well stepping over each drunken body passed out from a drunken binge. Each step praying we would not awaken them. The police bursting in, the hand cuffs that turned into hand shakes. Amazing how many people actually liked my dad!

I used to steal my dad's bullets and carry them to school. It was my only way of protecting my mother, brother and sister. That, started when he shot thru the house and missed my brother by only inches. Children shouldn't be afraid for the lives of their mother and siblings as well as their selves. He tried numerous times trying to run my mother and I over with his car. Once he almost succeeded in his deed. The car barreled down on us. We had nowhere to run, the car, suddenly stopped and stalled. He tried desperately to start it. Black smoke rolled out of the engine. Was this an intervention? It had to be otherwise we would probably both be dead, and that was not in the cards that night!

The older siblings were never told how badly things had gotten, there was nothing they could do anyway. So we toughed it out the best we could. Mom worked nights and we rarely got to see her, even she couldn't know the things we endured. It would just be more worry on her and God know she didn't need anymore on her!

One night after a blow out at home, my sister and her husband took me to Ohio to live. I stayed with them for awhile, got a job and then came home to a list of chores to do before I could call it a night. Only problem was, I was getting nowhere. I worked eleven hours a day, came home fixed supper for their kids. Cleaned up after them bathed them and put them to bed. I also cleaned their house and took out the trash and handed over my pay check at the end of the week. In a way, in turn for living there I became their slave. With no money to ever possibly get on my feet, I knew this wasn't going to be such a good idea.

My sister and her husband both worked nights. The nursery was at the top of the stairs, my make shift room consisted of a bed on the landing and their room was behind my make shift area. I would often have visions of a necklace of some sort with a jewel swinging back and forth in front of my face. It never made sense to me. I had had many visions before, some were just brief. Some would be re-occurring ones that didn't make sense. Some would come as warnings I guess, but at the time didn't recognize them as such.

The swinging of the necklace was chalked up to an old Vincent Price movie I had recently watched on the television. It did seem odd to me that after I somewhat rationalized it, that it happened more often. It was as if I were missing something, or a warning of some kind.

I was simply over worked and probably visualized it in hopes it would be an axe! Since I hadn't had bloody dreams for awhile, I softened it with a red jewel! Maybe it was my way of cutting into the situation I was now in, metaphorically speaking "Cutting my way out!"

My brother-in-law would sometimes come home early. He would make crashing sounds downstairs as if a burglar were entering. He wanted to make sure I would be awakened. Then he would creep up the stairway casting a huge shadow on the walls from the street light in front of the house.

Each step he took was with a heavy and deliberate stomp. I was in the open there was nowhere to hide, the children were in harm's way and I couldn't get to them! I jumped out of bed and grabbed the flashlight ready to bash his head open, suddenly I realized it was him! I got back in bed and pretended to have never heard a sound!

Next time he did his little scare tactic I was ready for him! I heard the familiar noises as he entered. I had already rigged the stairwell and was ready for his heavy footsteps to echo on the stairs. I crouched down by the banister and the next step he took I pulled up on the wire I had strung across the step. He tripped and I threw a bucket of water over his head, he then fell down the steps! Let's just say he never done it again.

Anyway things were not working out and one night I came home, I had once again had enough! He had pretty much quit working leaving my sister to go to school, and work while he sat doing nothing. My list grew larger and his demands, were variable getting unrealistic. I was tired of never being able to have a life and taking care of everyone else. We argued about the kids, both with snotty noses, gated in on the porch, barefooted and cold. My sister in bed trying to get a little sleep before her ten-hour shift. I took care of the kids and went out the door with a small bag and never went back!

I had nowhere to go so I walked the streets that night, I was tired and thoughts ran thru my head. I sat down on a bus bench to rest a few minutes. After a short while I started walking again. I was just about to give up when I found a prize! A rather large box in an alley behind a staircase. It would do nicely! The best part was it was not occupied! I lived in that box for a week and two days. I washed up at a local gas station and ate lunch at the nursery each day as I had no money for dinner. I lived in that grand old box which I was rather fond of, after all it was a place to sleep! I received my pay check and looked for an apartment.

I felt bad for my sister but every time I called to talk to her I ended up hanging up as he would answer the phone. She had no idea where I was or why I left. I found a small efficiency apartment ironically in the same building I found shelter under the stairs! Talk about fate my box still stood waiting for me. Someone else could have it now as I would leave it for the need of a homeless person less fortunate than I. After all I did have a job, just no money!

There were five apartments all upstairs a key was required to gain access to the stairwells that led to the apartments. I felt safer than I had felt in a long time. My apartment consisted of two rooms. A living slash bedroom and a small kitchen. The bathroom was located for use of all, at the end of the hall. Lucky for me it was right next to my apartment.

The knocking started the very first night I moved in. Three knocks on the door. The sofa was right next to the door so in a split second I could open it without even getting up. But, no one was ever there. Funny how when the knocks would come, the lights would flicker. I thought it odd that I never saw any one in passing going or coming from the bathroom. I never even heard the door opening or shutting or a flush. I decided maybe they actually did have bathrooms in their apartments, but it wouldn't explain the lack of toilet paper or water rings in the tub if that were the case. Very odd, I never heard a television or saw a light underneath anyone's door. Well, maybe all the apartments weren't rented after all.

One night I actually heard someone just outside my door. I got up slowly and peeked thru the key hole to see who was there. I could hear whispering and slight footsteps. The hall exposed all the apartments, but I saw no one! Then a loud bang hit up against my door and sent me to the floor. I didn't see anything! There was no one outside my door! I was a bit baffled, "What the heck!" I said under my breath as I picked myself up off the floor! Then I heard footsteps running down the hall! I swung the door open as I heard a door slam shut!

It came from the front apartment. The biggest of all the apartments. I looked down at the bottom of the door hoping to at least see a light. I saw a soft glow as if perhaps a candle were lit then I heard the meowing of a cat, but not just one cat it sounded like several! There were no animals allowed or so I was told. I shook my head and closed my door. Maybe that's why she stays to herself, she doesn't want anyone to know of her cats and she's weird!

I fell asleep about midnight that night strange dreams came to me and I awoke coughing with the strong smell of smoke! I jumped up thinking the building must be on fire. I felt the door for heat, once I was convinced it was okay to open the door, I yanked it open. I was prepared to yell "FIRE" to get the attention of the other tenants, "If there were any". When I was surprised to find all was clear, no smell of smoke engulfed me as it had a few minutes before. My throat was still burning from the attack I had just had with the fathom smoke. I closed the door and got a glass of water. I suppose I could have been dreaming, however the evidence was very real. My eyes and throat were a sure bet that I had actually been thru a burning of something!

The strange phone calls started shortly after that. The phone would ring, I would answer, I would hear heavy breathing, a low growl and sometimes a whisper I couldn't quite make out. I chalked them up to prank calls until one night the calls wouldn't stop! One right after the other, there was simply no time for anyone to have time to dial the number! We didn't have call back in those days. I finally just took the receiver off the hook and laid it on the floor. I went to bed only to be awakened by a loud ringing of the telephone, which lay at my feet still off the hook!

I was shocked, I slowly picked up the receiver, I placed it back on the phone and unplugged it from the wall. A loud bang hit against the wall and footsteps once again could be heard scurrying down the hall. A door slammed, I knew there was no need looking out, all was once again quiet.

A few days all was good. No knocks, no strange calls, no smoke and no banging on the wall, even the electric seemed to even itself out.

It was a Friday night I made it home just in time for a sudden thunderstorm to burst from the sky. The lights flickered and the thunder roared. I found the candles just in time for the lights to go out. I fixed myself a sandwich when a flash of lighting lit up the sky, and something caught my eye. I walked over to the window overlooking the back yard and alley. It was so dark and the rain pounded against the window. I was thankful I was inside safe and warm, and not huddled under the stairs in a wet cardboard box! It was hard to see anything. I started to walk away when another blast lit up the sky. I could see a figure of a person standing facing the alley, arms reaching outward. The rain beat down and the thunder and lighting became louder. It didn't seem to bother the woman. She wore a long dress and some sort of shawl, her hair long and unruly. She seemed to be yelling something, but with the downpour beating hard against the windowpane and roof, combined with the crashing and rumbling of thunder and cracking of lighting it was impossible to hear anything else!

I stood watching her, mesmerized by her gestures and the lightning that surrounded her. It didn't seem to bother her at all. I pulled up a chair and started eating my sandwich as I watched. All of a sudden she turned quickly and pointed up at me! I practically fell out of my chair as I veered away from her view. How did she know I was watching her! I chanced a peek, peering from the bottom of the window pain.

A flash of lighting revealed, "She was gone!" I breathed a sigh of relief, yet wondered where she had gone so fast. A sudden cold chill crept up my body and my candle went out! A picture fell off the wall as a loud bang hit somewhere in the hall. I lit my candle and started toward the living area. I stepped on something wet as I walked barefoot thru the room. Oh great I thought a leak. I held the candle toward the ceiling trying to see where to set a bucket. No sign of a leak, I stepped again, another wet spot. I lowered the candle toward the floor. Alarm shot thru my body, not only was the floor wet the puddles were clearly footprints! Footprints leading to the front door which to my surprise was cracked open!

I quickly scanned the small room, the candlelight danced across the now bare walls. I ran to the door and scanned the hallway. Nothing no puddles of water, no footprints only the shadows of the light sconces dancing in unison with the flickering of the candle. My heart was beating so fast I thought it would never calm down! I closed the door and locked it I put a knife in the frame. I was positive I had locked it before, it was the first thing I always done, strange, but perhaps with the brewing of the storm and hurrying home I guess it's possible I could have left it open. I slept with one eye open so to speak so by morning I was exhausted. I was glad it was my day off.

Things were quiet for a few days and I actually caught a glimpse of one of my neighbors, and managed a short conversation. She had moved in a month prior to me. She didn't stay there much as she and her boyfriend had gotten engaged right after she rented the apartment. I asked her about the other tenants. Margret a middle aged lady worked as an aid and often spent nights at different clients houses. Another had recently been sent to a nursing home as her health was failing. When I asked about the last tenant she pulled me inside her room and quietly closed her door.

She stood close to me and whispered as though she were afraid the woman would hear her. Her apartment was right next to hers. Her eyes grew wider as she spoke.

"That one is very peculiar!" She began. "She really frightens me." At night when I first moved in I could hear running up and down the hallway all night long. When I would peak out I couldn't see anyone! Then a loud bang would hit up against my door and scare me terribly!"

"I've never seen a light under her door, just the flickering of candle light."" I hear her saying strange things, and although pets are not allowed it sounds like she has lots of cats!" "The other night when it was storming, I saw her!" She seemed to be dancing and singing or praying or something there in the alley!" I saw her out the bathroom window, I think she saw me I got scared I ran as fast as I could back to my room!"

We continued to talk, she too had had strange calls and heard strange things. I asked her if she remembered when she ran to her room that night if she saw if my door was open. Unfortunately she was in such a state that no she didn't. She told me that she had many strange dreams when she would stay in her apartment. She was so glad she was now moving, and advised me to do the same.

It was mainly just the two of us now, I couldn't afford to move so I would just be cautious. The nightmares started, the crazy lady continued to knock and run down the hall. The phone calls continued. I was bound and determined she would not run me out.

Funny once I accepted the way it was it didn't bother me that much. I would come home at night and knock once on her door yell I'm home now. Then head to my room and turn the television up to drown out all the bangs and knocks and such. Months passed things got quiet. I barely knew she was still there.

One day I came home and her door was wide open. I peeked in from the hall. The room was empty! I was very surprised, I walked in and snooped around hoping she had left a clue to who and what she was. There were claw marks on the furniture and drapes indicating she indeed had cats!

The rug had melted candle wax splattered about and there was somewhat of a marking or drawing of which couldn't be made out as it was all scratched and seemed to be somewhat sanded to hide its origin. There was some kind of powder in a bowl next to a small table. The room smelt funny and I became uncomfortable. I left the room. I was glad she was gone and didn't care where she went.

I had strange dreams of her in the rain that night, dancing about and reaching into the darkness. A blast of lighting and a crack of thunder shook the building. I jumped up wide awake. I ran to the kitchen and peeked thru the drops of rain splattered window pane. I breathed a sigh of relief when there was no sign of her. Just a dream, I went back to bed and slept peacefully the rest of the night.

The next night when I arrived home I was surprised to hear noises coming from her apartment! Wow they rented it quickly I said to myself as I unlocked my door. I fixed my dinner, watched a little television, then went down to take a shower. I would be nice to have a neighbor that may be home once in awhile.

I decided to clean the tub extra good and just soak for awhile, relax and listen to some music. I knew I couldn't stay long since it was after all a shared bathroom. None the less I would make the best of it. Bubbles in, earplugs on music to ease my soul. I had settled in just starting to relax when I thought I heard someone knock on the door. I pulled the earplugs out, I thought I heard the familiar sound of a cat meowing just outside my door. I hope she didn't forget one of her cats I said under my breath. I hurried and finished my bath. Cleaning the tub I suddenly felt as though I were not alone. I gathered my things and headed out the door, I suddenly stopped in my tracks.

The familiar glow of candlelight danced beneath the door. I listened for sounds, I tiptoed down the hall towards her door. Someone was coming up the stairs, I made a quick exit into the safety of my room. I peeked out thru the key hole, but couldn't see anyone. I'm just being paranoid I told myself after all I light candles myself. New tenant, new home probably making it smell good. No sign of a cat, probably my imagination.

Everything was peaceful. No noises, all was good. Work went well the next day and I managed to get home in time to see my landlord closing up his office which was beneath the apartments. I mentioned the new tenant. He looked surprised.

"There are no tenants except for you and Louise. Maxine moved out two days ago. So, Maxine was in the front apartment I asked?

"Oh, no that is Louise."

"She has lived there for probably twenty five years or more." He said.

"Didn't she move out a couple days ago? Her apartment was empty, I went inside, the door was open." I said.

"No I'm positive, I spoke with her, she will never move out." He said.

I was confused, as I unlocked the security door and started up the stairs to my apartment. I passed in front of her door I could hear her laughing almost hysterically. I hurried to my apartment and once inside locked the door securely behind me.

I began evaluating my own sanity. Convinced I was not insane, I made dinner and sat in front of the television. I fell asleep shortly after that. Laughing, came from somewhere in the hall interrupting my sleep. The banging started and the knocks on the door began. The phone rang, I grabbed it. Laughing came from inside the phone! I put my hands over my ears as the noises became so loud it seemed to shake the building!

I had had enough! I swung the door open and screamed at the top of my lungs!

"STOP IT!"

"STOP IT YOU DAMMED OLD HAG!" "I'M NOT AFRAID OF YOU!" I WILL NOT BE RAN OUT OF MY HOME!"

The lights flickered in the hall threatening to go out. The noises came to an abrupt stop all was quiet. I stepped back inside and slammed the door. I waited expecting the worst. All remained quiet.

Several days passed everything was extremely calm. I kept waiting on her to do something crazy. Then it dawned on me. Here I am waiting on her next move while she sits and laughs knowing in her strange twisted way she won again!

Oddly enough months went by and I hardly ever heard a sound out of the ordinary. We had I guess reached an understanding in a strange sort of way. The candle light could still be seen underneath the door, indicating she was still around. It was wonderful coming home and actually sleeping all night without the banging and carrying on. The phone did still ring but someone was always on the other end!

I lived there for a little over a year, funny I never laid eyes on her except for that stormy rainy night in the alley. It was time to move when I received a call from my brother, he was coming home from his hitch in Viet Nam. With just a small area it would never work. He stayed with my sister when he first arrived until we found a place big enough for both of us. Meanwhile I had introduced him to a friend, which later became his wife.

Trouble seemed to always find me, so when I moved away from the apartment I grew to love. It was only to open another door to the unknown and face yet another chapter in my life. Only this time I wasn't alone.

THE PLAQUE

The apartment my brother and I rented on Main Street in Dayton, Ohio was a second floor apartment. The first thing I noticed about it was how dark the stairwell was as well as the hall way. The inside was not much lighter. It was fully furnished, the front door opened into the living room where a small sofa sat facing the door and somewhat in the middle of the room. It seemed to be used as a room divider as there were no other doors outside the bathroom door in the entire apartment. The kitchen was located in the back of the apartment separated only by the bedroom wall. Very crazy layout.

The day we came to look at it we found the landlady to be a little strange not to mention nosey. As she walked us thru the small but spacious two bedroom apartment she started asking questions. It wasn't the normal questions a landlord would ask, it was more on a personal level.

It was almost as if I weren't even there. She asked him if I would ever be alone and for how long and when he would be home. She asked what time he would be leaving for work as well as what time he would be home. She asked if he went out at night and left me for any length of time.

When my brother questioned her as to why she needed to know his coming's and going's she just said, "Oh, no reason, just it being so dark in halls and stairwells, new apartment settling noises and such."

Then it was a quick jerk of her head as she turned to look at me for the first time acknowledging the fact I was indeed there. She had a kind of crazed look about her, I began to question her stability.

Had we not been desperate for a place to live we certainly would have left at that point! She then said, "Is she afraid to be alone?"

My brother was getting a little agitated at this point and merely stated, "I just came back from Viet Nam, I'm pretty handy with a gun. If anything were to mess with either of us, rest assured I would take care of it!" "As far as she goes she can handle a gun pretty well herself and carries one. I'm not too worried. She's been taught to shoot and ask questions later."

At that point she handed him the key and as she started toward the door she turned and said, "it's not a gun you will need!" She laughed as she went out the door. I followed her to the door, locked it, then shot a glance at my brother I rolled my eyes and shrugged my shoulders. He laughed as we started cleaning.

"Nice touch, the she can handle a gun pretty well, and carries one!" I laughed. "Yeah, I thought so!" Then added, "Well maybe word will get out and at least no one will mess with you!"

We moved in later that night, despite the wattage of the light bulbs the apt seemed very drab and darkish. We heard noises throughout the night and decided we must have rats as well as crazy neighbors. We vowed to get rat traps and look for a better place to live.

My brother and his girlfriend had been home all day when I came in from work that evening. It was raining pretty hard and made the apartment that much darker regardless of the lighting. The flash of the lightning was a welcome sight giving the room an added blast of light.

Another flash of lightning revealed a large shadow that appeared to be swinging back and forth from the kitchen. A sudden cold breeze came from the darkened kitchen. I assumed a window was open causing the curtain to cast a shadow as the fierce wind blew it back and forth.

I turned on the light, the room was still a little cool but no windows were open and nothing to cause a shadow. There was a large tree outside so I decided it must have been a branch blowing in the fierce wind.

We sat around talking for a while as the storm continued to rage. The crash of thunder shook the apartment. A few minutes later flashing red lights raced by with sirens blaring, lightning had struck somewhere near. It was obvious the storm wasn't ready to subside any time soon, so it was no shocker that when my brother had to take his girlfriend home I opted to stay alone.

The electricity flickered on and off several times as I sat there on the sofa. I knew it was senseless to look for a flashlight or for that matter even a candle. Those were things on my list I had yet to purchase. Funny, how you don't think of things like that until you need them.

I sat there for what seemed an eternity, it had been a long day at work and I really just wanted to take a shower and call it a day. With the storm still raging I wasn't about to get into the shower and take a chance on the electricity going out so I waited it out.

I leaned back thinking maybe a short nap would be good and my brother would soon return. I closed my eyes for just a second when I felt a light tap on my shoulder. Knowing I was alone I sat straight up! I quickly turned to look behind me, nothing was there. I turned back around and leaned back again. A few seconds later another tap. I quickly turned again and looked behind me, this time I got on my knees and looked to see if someone was squatted down behind the sofa. No one was there. The television wasn't on so I sat there staring at it. I would use the black screen as a reflecting device; I would spot any intruder before he would have a chance to do any harm.

I knew my brother had been home all day if someone had been there they would have been discovered long before now. Then I shuddered to think perhaps a mouse had been on my shoulder. A loud bang came from the kitchen just as a loud crack of thunder and a blast of lightning lit up the room. Damn rats I thought, come on where are you? I said under my breath.

I shook it off as just nerves and a slight giggle escaped my mouth as I once again sat back and tried to relax. It wasn't long before another tap came on my right shoulder, it was an unmistakable tap a lot harder than the previous ones. This was no rat, I started to turn when a grip on my left shoulder sent me running for the door!

No need to look back! I needed to get as much distance between myself and the perpetrator as possible! I don't know where he had been hiding and I wasn't about to ask him now! Truth is I had a gun, but could I really use it on anyone? Running seemed to be a better option and since I was home my gun was in my room inside my purse, so I guess I would never know if I would have pulled the trigger had the circumstance been different. One thing I was sure of this girl could RUN! And run I did!

The flash of lightning lit up the darkened sky as I ran. The thunder was crashing so loud I didn't know if my perpetrator was on my heels. Just run faster I told myself, as the rain was coming down so violently I could hardly see! The puddles of standing water splashed up my legs as I ran. I was surprised to not see any cars going down the road as it was on a busy street.

I had ran for what seemed to be miles, I was out of breath and couldn't go another step. A bus bench was just on the corner I chanced a look behind me, a flash of lightning revealed I was alone. I stumbled over to the bench, cold, wet and out of breath.

A car came down the road and about the same time the light changed to red. I ran and jumped in the passenger side of the car, nearly scaring my brother to death! "Dutchie!" He said unsure of really who I was at that point, he left me at home remember, he certainly never expected to see me on the corner in the pouring rain!

"Jesus, you scared the shit out of me! It reminded me of the old twilight zone episode where the dead girl is in the pouring rain trying to get home!"

We had only lived in the apartment a couple days. I didn't care if we ever went back after all that. I told him about the intruder. When we arrived back home the door was still wide open just as I left it. We searched the apartment finding nothing.

A neighbor poked his head out from the safety of his apartment. My brother asked him if he saw anyone leaving our apartment. He said "Nope, he never leaves, just scares people. He don't mean nothing by it."

It was at that moment we were informed a man had hung himself in the kitchen! The shadow I saw must have been him after all. My brother and I sat on the sofa, I listened as he told me of shadows he had seen and sounds he had heard over the last few days. He didn't tell me because he didn't want to scare me. Truth was, I was more afraid of what I thought was a real live person hiding in the house, than I would have been if I had known it was a ghost. I was certainly no stranger to them, but after all, how could he have known as I hadn't discussed any of my secrets with anyone.

A few days later his girlfriend had spent the night and we were planning a trip to Indiana to visit my mom. She had rented a getaway apartment for my sister and her when my dad was on one of his binges. I had never been there before but, certainly knew where it was as it was located above the old strand theatre.

We went to bed early that night and I had had a dream. I was walking up some stairs that seemed to be made of hot tar as my feet seemed to sink into each step as I struggled to reach the top. Once at the top a long dark hallway lay in wait. In my dream the bathroom was not inside the apartment but down the hall. It was a very old building and as I walked down the hall to enter what in the dream must have been where I was living, the floor boards creaked underneath my feet. The hall had an eerie glow with the old time sconces mounted on the wall. The smell of the building filled my nostrils, something very old and musty.

I entered the apartment and one of my nieces sat on the sofa. She had gotten sick and I took her down the hall to the bathroom. She was throwing up and I was holding her hair back and reaching for a rag to wipe her face. That's when I saw the old lady. She was standing in the bathtub her long grey hair hanging wildly about her face and down the long black dress she was wearing. Her hands were inside her sleeves and she was just starring at us.

I screamed at her, "what are you starring at. Get out can't you see she's sick?" then it was as if I had forgotten all about my niece. The old lady seemed to capture my attention as she motioned me to follow her. I walked silently behind her, she seemed to float more than walk. She stopped at the opposite end of the hall not far from the staircase that led down to the main door. She opened a door that looked like a small closet.

A man sat at an old desk. He wore thick glasses and a white short sleeve shirt with suspenders to hold up his britches. An old lamp sat on the desk, it was a gold colored lamp with an old fashioned jade colored glass, molded in a sort of bowl like form for its shade. It reminded me of a lamp I once saw in an old western movie.

Not a word was spoken, it was as if we had some kind of understanding even though I had never seen the man before. He opened a drawer and pulled out a sort of plaque. He laid it on the desk and nodded toward me. I looked at the plaque it was charcoal in color and had five gold indentions to place my fingers on. It had words engraved in the plaque.

Without being spoken to or coaxed in any way. It was clear to me, I knew why I was there and what I was supposed to do. I placed my fingers onto the plaque and said the words that were engraved so solidly.

That's when I woke up! I was saying some kind of prayer and my hand was in the air fingers arched as if they were still on the plaque itself. Problem was I was still saying the prayer when I woke up!

I will never forget it as I still remember it as clearly as if it were yesterday. I knew it had to have a meaning, something significant to it, a deep embedded secret meaning of some kind!

"With this hand I place on this prayer, lead me, teach me to where there is no wrong!"

My brother and his girlfriend were standing in the door way looking at me, both with a confused look on their faces.

"That was some crazy shit!" They both said at the same time.

"It was as if you were chanting, saying it over and over again."

They were surprised to find I was alone in the room. They both heard someone else talking as well as me!

I couldn't shake the crazy dream, it was just to real, to vivid. It had a meaning, and I knew I would never forget it. Odd thing was a few years later I would find out, leaving me more confused than ever!

I started telling them about the crazy dream as we drove down the highway. My brother and his girlfriend both had had a crazy dream that night. It was as if we all had a messed up night of unrest.

When we arrived at my mom's apartment, we entered the doorway to a staircase that went straight up. As we stepped unto the staircase and headed up I had a familiar feeling come over me. My feet felt like they were sinking and it was hard to walk up the stairs. I noticed both my brother and his girlfriend seemed to be having the same problem.

We started giggling a little at the thought of what we would see when we reached the top, as it was like the steps I described in the dream. When we finally reached the top we all three stood at a complete halt.

Oh, my God the hall was just as I said it was. I told them the bathroom should be on the left as we walk down the hall if it's the same as my dream.

We grabbed a hold of each other's arm as we carefully walked toward the end of the hall. We stopped short when we peered into an open doorway revealing "The bathroom!" We squealed as we ran to the end of the hall seeing a familiar face peek out from the doorway at the noise we were making.

Once at the door I chanced a look behind me, wondering if the old lady would make an appearance. The hall was long and dark but no sign of her. Little did I know then that I would be moving back and living in the place my dream was made from.

THE HOUSE NO ONE WANTED

It was a beautiful old two story house sitting on a corner lot. It had made someone a fine home back in the day. I would see people move in and then a few weeks later move out. A small one bedroom apartment had been made at the far corner of the house. I walked past the house in Dayton Ohio, many times and guessed the rent to be pretty high.

Finally it was empty again, I knew I probably couldn't afford it but I just wanted to see inside. It was great! It was just the right size for me and I was surprised to find it was cheaper than my last apartment! My brother and his new bride were living with me at the time, but had made plans to move back to Indiana.

The tenants had not yet moved their things and I was told they would get them by Friday and I could move in. I was due to go on vacation with some friends to Virginia Beach that Friday, so my brother agreed to move for me. They would stay until I returned home.

When I returned it was late, the lights were all out and no one had lived in the larger side of the house for a very long time. I was surprised to find I could not get into the house and my brother was not home. I finally found one of the windows open just a crack so I managed to climb in.

It was a little creepy it was dark and I wasn't familiar with where the light switches were located. Once the lights were on I found a note from my brother. They had moved, sorry they weren't here when I arrived, here's your key. They had at least moved my stuff in, but I was surprised to find the other tenants things were still there!

It was odd that their suitcases were packed and ready to go, there food was still in the cabinets and refrigerator. It looked as though they had left in a hurry. I was just settling in getting ready to clean the place up a bit when the phone rang. It was my friend Julie, she was having a restless night and asked if I would go out with her for awhile. She picked me up a short time later. We weren't gone long and when we returned I invited her in to see my new place.

I told her about the tenants leaving their things and I was a bit concerned that they may still have a key. She advised me to lock up tight and maybe put a knife in the door until the landlord could put a new lock on. She left shortly afterwards. I was really tired so I took a shower and went to bed.

The living room sat in the front of the house, a small hallway where the bathroom and bedroom sat directly across from each other, then a small step down was the kitchen. The bedroom had thick carpet and it was hard to shut the door. Since I was concerned the tenants would come back I pushed it shut. I was a pretty light sleeper and it would give me just enough time to protect myself if the need arose.

I had just laid down when I heard a click, and a small beam of light show thru the door from the bathroom! I had just checked everything! All the doors were locked! The door started opening a little further. I grabbed the phone in one hand and my gun in the other! I was out of bed in a flash standing and waiting! I had nowhere to run I was ready to fight!

I heard the water in the bathroom faucet come on. It had a certain sound like metal rubbing as the rusty faucet was turned on. It to was a little hard to turn on. What the hell was going on! No one came in so I went out! The water had been turned on and was filling up the sink, I turned it off and started turning the lights on as I did a walk thru.

Somehow I knew I would not be alone yet, no one was there. The answer to why the house stayed empty was clear. I knew the tenants left in a hurry and I knew at that moment they would not be back! Satisfied no one, that was living that is, was hiding anywhere I went back to bed. I shut the door securely behind me. Tomorrow I would move my television set into the bedroom, tonight I just wanted to sleep!

A friend was over the following evening she and her boyfriend had been arguing, she needed a place to stay for the night. I told her nothing about my "ghost" as they were not really strangers to me. It was just that I didn't know this spirit so I was a little on guard.

We went over to the chicken place to get dinner, it was just across the street, no need to lock the door or turn the television off. When we returned we sat down to eat. We were enjoying the show and talking as we ate when the television screen went totally black. The first thing I thought was the picture tube had blown out. The sound grew louder on the television as I came closer to it. The room became icy cold even though it was summer time. The old wicker rocking chair that I had purchased at an antique store a year ago started to rock back and forth!

I was astonished to find that the brightness had been turned all the way down on the television and the sound all the way up! By this time Linda is right next to me eyes wide mumbling something to me as if she couldn't speak.

I myself was a little overwhelmed at that point. We stood in the middle of the room knowing it was watching us probably laughing and enjoying the prospect that we would soon flee as the others had done. That may have been so, but at the time we couldn't seem to move!

The telephone rang and jolted me back to reality cause this wasn't real, was it? The rocking had stopped, the television was back to normal. The temperature of the room was warmer. Whatever was there was now gone, at least for now.

She looked so scared as we stood there in the room holding on to each other. Then I started to laugh it was a nervous laugh and she soon joined in. "What the hell was that? It scared the shit out of me!" She said.

The phone was still ringing, funny how it jolted us back to the norm, we forgot to answer it with all the confusion! It started ringing again, we both ran over to answer it a little apprehensive to be separated by more than a few inches!

It was my boyfriend Rick. He was in the neighborhood and was it okay to come by. He arrived a short time later. He pulled up to the curb a thought popped into my head out of nowhere. "Don't let him in the house!" Suddenly and for absolutely no reason I became afraid for him!

I wasn't sure why the thought came to me, but I was uneasy and decided we would just sit outside for a bit then maybe go for a drive. We sat there for a while, traffic had slowed down, the chicken place had closed, the noises from inside the house were now obvious. I told him the television was still on, but the look on Linda's face made him take note. "You okay?" He said. She gave me a nervous look, I smiled, she nodded yes. Then added she was just tired. I gave her a look of thanks as I wasn't ready to reveal the things that were happening. I didn't know how he would take it. I would tell him in time, but not now.

He left a short time after that and we reluctantly went inside. Things seemed to have settled down as we went into the kitchen for a late night snack. We left the kitchen each carrying a small saucer of cookies and a cup of milk. We got as far as the step when a loud bang came from behind us! Then very loud heavy footsteps, as though something were running behind us! Needless to say a scream escaped from both of us at the exact same time, sending echoes from the narrow hallway. We both jumped and ran bumping into each other as we scurried toward the bedroom. Cookies went flying and milk splattered all over the walls! Another bang sent us into the nearest doorway! Only problem was she ended up in the bedroom and I in the bathroom!

Each of us thinking at the time something (got) the other one! I sank to the floor pressing my back against the door. I was panting for breath, I could hear the pounding of my heartbeat. Everything was quiet now. I peeked thru the keyhole. Noticing the bedroom door was shut tightly, I called out to Linda, hoping she would hear me. A sob came from across the hall.

"Are you okay?" I asked. Her voice was a little shaky.

"I have to pee!" She said thru her tears. I couldn't help but giggle a little. I cracked the door open and instructed her to do the same. All seemed to be clear, I told her to open her door and run into the bathroom. It was directly across the hall just a few steps. I opened my door and she slammed hers shut crying, "I can't."

"It's okay, I'll come and get you." "Open your door and take my hand." I stepped into the hall keeping my eyes on the darkened kitchen. Her hand touched mine and we ran back into the safety of the bathroom!

It proved to be a very long night, we stood by the bathroom door listening. Waiting for our chance to run to the bedroom. We stood very still, we stood very quiet. Both our ears to the door, holding onto each other's hand for safety. You could have heard a pin drop. I cracked the door open just enough to peek out with one eye. All of a sudden the water came on in the sink behind us! It startled me and I slammed the door shut! Oh hell no, I realized my mistake as Linda screamed in my ear! I struggled trying to open the door with her pushing up against me. At that moment we were our own worst enemy! We couldn't get out! Finally I pushed her back enough to get the door cracked open. She grabbed it and swung it open busting me in the head as she ran out! I struggled to my feet, blood trickling down my face. I couldn't see for a moment I was dazed! That dam door was hard! I no longer reached the hall when something grabbed my arm and pulled me into the bedroom!

She was in tears now and shaking uncontrollably, as she held onto me. I couldn't yet think straight and my head was really hurting. We sank to the floor our backs against the wall. I wiped the blood from my face, I wasn't sure what to do! I knew that if he was able to get into the bathroom, he could also very well be in the very same room as we were! Watching us, playing with us, laughing at us! I didn't want to cause further alarm to Linda, I knew there was no place to hide, so I said nothing. We lost track of time as the night grew into morning. We had both fallen asleep at one point or at least she did. I probably had a concussion and passed out. Nonetheless all remained quiet and nothing else had happened.

When we woke up, she couldn't wait to get out and gladly go back to her boyfriend. She said nothing could ever be that bad between them to make her ever come to my house again! She looked at the dried blood on my head and face and the huge knot. "Oh my God!" " What happened to you!" She asked as concern covered her face. I smiled "It's okay, I just ran into the door!" There was no point in telling her what she did. She was to upset and it was an accident, plus she did come back for me!

It was my home and I had dealt with ghost before, just not on this level. I made up my mind it was not going to chase me away! It was a big house we would just have to work something out. I had a plan.

I decided I had enough friends that they could take turns staying with me! Most of them were single so it shouldn't pose a problem. Provided Linda wouldn't tell them what happened. However even if she did they may not believe her, and they were curious, so chances were still good.

Sure enough the events took place pretty regularly. Footsteps and shadows were the newest Happenings. The television, the rocking chair, cold spots, the banging, the water and the doors opening on their own continued on a nightly basis. I was getting somewhat used to it in a strange kind of way.

Friends came and friends went. We had some funny moments, and some very scary moments and moments when my friends would flee in the middle of the night! I soon ran out of friends. It didn't make any difference if it was day or night anymore. I would just have to stay alone.

I knew one thing for certain I could never tell my family. I knew if I did they would either think I was crazy or try and convince me to move in with them for a while. I was a big girl and I could take care of myself! Besides if it scared me to death, I would be tied to the house forever, as it was, I had nowhere else to go! After all, the house had a history and many secrets that's probably one reason I stayed. I had been fascinated with it long before I ever moved in and it was a beautiful old house. Remember the rent was cheap and therefore I was meant to live there. It was like it drew me in, enticed me, called out to me in a strange way. Making me want it and now even with all that had taken place, I really loved the house!

My friend Julie and her husband were leaving for vacation and asked me to feed her cats while she was away. My older sister Kira and her husband were planning a night out with my sister Kylie and her husband. Kylie had to work late that night but they were going to meet at my house as I had agreed to babysit all five of the children.

Jake and Kira arrived first with their three children. Kevin dropped the other two children off shortly after they arrived. I was glad I had moved the television into the bedroom so the kids could watch it. Kira was getting them ready for bed while Jake drove me over to feed the cats. We were only gone a short time, but I guess it was an eternity to a very shaken and frightened Kira stood on the front steps crying when we returned.

Jake jumped out of the car and ran over to her. "What's wrong?" he asked over and over again. She was to shaken to speak. I replied I think I know, I turned to Kira and tried to calm her down. She held on to my hands as she explained what had taken place.

She had put the kids to bed and turned on the television. They were pretty tired and fell asleep as soon as she covered them up. She turned the television off and shut the door. A few minutes later she could hear the television come on. Thinking it was one of the kids she went to check on them.

Before she got to the bedroom door the sound blasted out from the television full volume. She struggled to open the door. She said it was as if someone were holding it shut. When she was able to get in, she discovered all five children were fast asleep! The television had swirling circles coming from it, she felt like it was drawing her in. The sound went very low and she felt very cold and venerable. She freaked out! She just knew she had to get out, she turned to check on the kids. All five children sleeping peacefully. All of a sudden the volume went full blast sending her running out the door! She was to frightened to go back inside.

"You left the kids inside!" I said, as I ran past her into the room afraid of what I may find. They were sleeping soundly all the racket didn't seem to phase them at all. We finally coaxed Kira back into the house.

Kylie and Kevin had arrived about this time. I was forced to tell them what had been taking place over the past few months. As I was telling my story, Rick had arrived. We had to start all over again as we filled him in on what had happened.

He sat in my antique rocker, my sisters and I sat on the sofa next to each other. Kevin stood by the door and Jake sat on the chair close to the door. Someone decided it would be good to have a séance. "What in the hell were we thinking!"

I didn't want to but, Rick assured me it would be okay. I trusted him so I finally agreed. We all sat holding hands, the candle sat in the middle of the coffee table. We closed our eyes and someone began to speak. I felt as if someone were behind me gently pulling my hair causing my head to lean back. I opened my eyes to see that Kira was doing the same thing! She looked at me and we both mentioned it to the others. About the same time I glanced into the kitchen, Kira saw it about the same time. A hideous face seem to glare at us in warning, I felt he was angry because I told!

My eyes were glued for a second, I couldn't believe what I was clearly looking at. I had a sudden urge to get the hell out of dodge! Kira started shaking and a cry escaped her throat. Odd thing was we both had a stain like old blood on our hands after that, and ironically in the same position on our hands! Whatever it was it just wouldn't wash off.

Boy! The things I let people talk me into. Rick convinced me to face it head on and see what it wanted. He knew as well as I that I would have to live there and we needed to "understand" each other. Was I stupid or something!?

We sat back down after we investigated the kitchen to see if perhaps it was a reflection or something or perhaps someone peeking in the window. We hadn't discussed exactly what we saw just a hideous face.

We held hands and were instructed to concentrate. Not to break the chain, someone once again asked the questions. Rick's hand started feeling very cold, so cold I couldn't resist I had to open my eyes. I looked over at him as I held his frigid hand, I was out of there! Over the table without touching it, Jake grabbed me as I ran past almost knocking him over. He was no match for me. He couldn't hold me, I was out the door as Kevin grabbed me, he too couldn't hold me! I weighed all of ninety pounds but when adrenaline kicks in it kicks ass!

Fear that went through my body gave me superman strength! They were no match for me! Rick was out the door as were the others. He came closer to me, I backed away. I wanted nothing to do with him! "It was you! It was you all along!" I accused.

A squad car came around the corner about that time as Rick grabbed my arm trying to reason with me. The officer got out of the car to investigate, that's when we told him the bazaar story from the beginning. I just knew he thought we were all on drugs.

He surprised me by telling us he had had several calls through the years of strange things happening in this house. He was very interested. He came into the house with his partner. They questioned everyone. Officer John took me into the kitchen while his partner Carl took Kira into the living room. They were most interested in what we had seen.

Ironically we both drew a picture so similar there was no question we had both indeed witnessed "his" appearance. The Officers patrolled more often and gave me their personal phone numbers in case anything happened. They wanted to witness for themselves as it was also an interest they had had for a long time. I certainly felt better knowing they understood and were willing to come if I needed them.

I soon reasoned that the entity was coming through Rick, but I didn't want to be that close ever again so no more séance were allowed! I lived there for several months after that. Nothing major happened, but the bedroom door would still come open at night. The faucet would come on and he still liked playing with the television, cold spots, footsteps everything was the same, the loud bangs always startled me the most as they would always catch me off guard! Only thing different was I had a lot of nightmares!

My police officer friends spent some time at my apartment. They were mesmerized by the things that took place. One night, they were off duty of course, we snuck into the basement of the house. The musty smell was overpowering, the feeling that eyes followed us made it a little more exciting. It's funny how I felt so much braver with the two of them. A smile escaped my lips when I knew they were no more help than I. Actually I could probably protect, them truth be known. After all I had been haunted all my life and they were green horns so to speak. Firearms and brawn were no match to what we were up against! But, if the spirit of the lord lived with either of them, well then we would have a chance!

Antiques had been stored in the far corner by the stairs. There seemed to be an array of old mirrors and paintings leaning up against another wall. Carl leaned up against a wall and practically fell through! It was a hidden door! We stayed close as we entered. The flashlight scanned the room, no windows, it was clear what the room was used for. The drawings on the walls indicated some kind of rituals had been performed over the years. It was quite sickening to think they may even have sacrificed animals in the space. The pentagram on the floor somewhat faded as did the echo of the chants that once filled the room.

We discovered there had been several deaths over the years and although it was never proven two suicides and talk of one resident dealing in the occult. It was obvious it wanted to make its presence known. We could hear heavy footsteps above us and a door slammed somewhere in the distance. We quickly exited the basement.

They still came over from time to time mostly to check on me, another police officer, Paul an older man came a few times. He told me when he was a child he had heard the house was haunted. At Halloween one year he and a couple of his friends snuck into the basement. He said they heard noises like chanting and something flew across the room which sent them fleeing into the night! He said they never looked back until they reached the safety of their homes. They never went near the house again.

Everyone pressured me to move out. Since I had come to grips with what I had witnessed I was somehow not afraid anymore. I was more fascinated than anything. It had had a chance to do harm to me several times and it had not. Was I scared? Sure at first, then after learning of the occult rituals I became a little unnerved. Yes it was probably for the best that I move, I had heard of cases where it would only get worse. I decided I wasn't up for that! I lived there for almost a year, so I guess I did better than most. However moving out did not rid me of anything. Perhaps it only added to my crazy life! I knew there was no escape. I was used to it so it would come as no surprise when I would remain FOREVER HAUNTED!

THE MAN IN THE MIRROR

I had once again moved back to "Hell's hot spot!" I thought about my teenage years, as floods of memories engulfed me. True I was still a teenager of 18, but I had grown up in a hurry. My teen years at home as I recalled were rough as I struggled thru puberty and the teenage years in general. My identity was the biggest quest to overcome. I knew I was different from the other kids I just didn't seem to fit in properly. I wasn't an outcast, but I was somewhat of a loner and keep quiet for the most part.

I could keep secrets and a promise was sacred to me. A true friend was very hard to come by because I didn't trust anyone. There were things I could never tell even to my best friend. Things to horrible to ever mention. My secrets would remain secrets, they too would become memories I wish could forget, haunting memories echoing in my mind. Haunting me forever.

When I was a teenager I always thought something really bad was wrong with me. I would write short stories, only problem was the bad things in the stories would always seem to happen. I thought I was a witch. I would sometimes know what someone was going to say or do before they said or did it. Sometimes I would know who was calling before the phone even rang, or when someone was going to knock on the door. Often what someone was thinking, and sometimes I knew things had happened well before they actually happened! I had visions from time to time and sometimes I could feel the pain of an unseen presence. One vision I had was finding a dead man on the floor, another I saw a man drowning. Little did I know then that these events would take place in the not so distant future.

Sometimes I could see things, no one else could see. I sometimes had dreams that weren't dreams at all, they became real making me more and more confused. I thought I was the cause when things would be bad, after all, couldn't I have stopped them? Better yet, if I hadn't written about them would they have happened?!

On several occasions I avoided what could have been a very bad situation. Call it intuition or whatever I know I was protected by something. I could sometimes make objects move but it was usually when I was really angry or scared.

I always thought I didn't "fit in" with my family. Like maybe I was dropped on their doorstep or something and they were forced to take me. After all I was cute wasn't I?

I was and am so different from any of them even in my thinking. We don't share to many of the same interest and let's face it, I can communicate with the dead better than the living!

My mom, I really believe had a gift that probably frightened her for lack of understanding her talent. It would have been even worse for her back in the day. So I guess I would have done the same thing. After all I kept my secrets while I was growing up. But I really don't care what people think now. I know what I've seen and I know what I've heard and I definitely know what I've experienced!

My destiny was shaped long ago and prepared me for who I have become. I can remember scrying long before I knew what it was at an early age. I guess I never thought about it being dangerous. I would stand in front of the mirror and wish I looked like someone else. I would just stare into it for a while and my face would start to change. Only problem was my concentration would be broken with only one bathroom and seven other people needing in.

Privacy was unheard of in our house. I often felt alone even with so many around me all the time. No one seemed to understand me. I never even told my best friend Conny, for fear she wouldn't understand. I was definitely alone, but, in a way it just made me stronger. Spirits seemed to trust me perhaps because I didn't "tell" on them.

I wasn't afraid to be who I became. I simply laughed at their ignorance to deny what they couldn't explain. If they believed in God at all they would not be able to deny spirits as he is the greatest spirit I know. Then there's my favorite the Holy Ghost and didn't the bible say "The dead shall rise again!" It's all there plain and simple right before their eyes. Yet, they are blinded by fear. Frightened by the unknown, of an existing plain so close yet so far. I seemed to embrace their existence, run towards them while most run away. I do not understand the tie entirely, between them and me. I know we are linked in a way that time will unravel. In time I will know what they want of me, and I will know what I was put here to do, and I will succeed. Because in the end, they have been with me since birth. They have always been my guide. I just haven't fully embraced it.

I always felt that my dad was a little afraid of me. I think it was because I knew things about him, things he did. It was the way he looked at me on some occasions. Like once we were at the union hall and this woman was there, I didn't like her, and I was glaring at her. It made both of them very uncomfortable it was like something was going on and he knew that I knew. This happened several times on different occasions. He told me I was a witch one time and I never forgot it. It was as if he had confirmed what I had already knew.

I remember when my first vision of a man drowning happened. My dad and some of his friends had gone on a night fishing slash drinking binge. I remember when he came home that morning, the look on his face. I had never seen him look so bewildered. It was clear he cared about his friends way more than he ever did us. I overheard the conversation he had with my mother. Okay, I was ease dropping.

He told her his friend had fallen asleep while they were sitting around the campfire. He said he had a strange look on his face, screamed and ran into the water! It was very dark regardless of the stars and he went under. They just stood there peering into the darkness. There was no thrashing about, no struggle. The waters remained calm. It was as if nothing had disturbed the night. He was nowhere to be found.

They called it an accidental drowning. I often wondered about that, things just didn't add up. Something was not exactly as they said. When his friends would come over they whispered a lot and seemed to be worried about something. I wondered if he remembered me talking about the drowning man. He would look at me in a way like he was trying to figure out what else I knew. I only had suspicions and nothing more.

A year or so had passed when another friend, his very best friend died unexpectedly. He was devastated. My mother was out of town at the time and I was at the nursery school, where I worked.

I remember when he called he sounded so forlorn and lost. I couldn't help but feel sorry for him. It was a time in his life that alcohol had become his family and we really didn't matter. It was funny that he called me at the time because I was the last person he would have wanted to talk to. Perhaps it was the dead man on our kitchen floor that jolted something in his mind, after all didn't he know I was "Different!" Did he remember, yet something I had said a few years before?

After all was taken care of and the coroner was gone I had a feeling dad really wanted to tell me something. I could sense his discomfort in the way I looked at him. I still to this day knew there was more to it than what was being told. Oh, I don't mean like he actually murdered him or anything. But I felt that maybe on their drunken binge he felt guilty for not hearing the cries for help from his friend. In a way I know he felt responsible for his death. It wasn't the same feeling I had about the death of his fishing buddy. I had never seen him so weak and broken.

A few days later I was sitting reading a book in my apartment. It was a really small place with just the kitchen and living area which doubled as a bedroom. My dresser was in the closet area that had no door so I had a very clear view of the mirror.

Something caught my attention and I glanced up at the mirror. I was the only one in the room and the only one that could possibly make a reflection in the mirror, however something was wrong!

I got up and went over to the mirror. The girl that should have been me was not me! She resembled me, but it was not me. I touched my face to see what was wrong with me. I was a bit confused at what was happening. Before I could comprehend what was wrong with my face another face appeared in the place of mine.

The face was very familiar, I knew he had a message, I just wasn't sure how to obtain it. He was definitely trying to tell me something. I thought it strange that he would come to me and only his face was revealed, it was my dad's friend!

Well about that time the large closet door flew open over the kitchen sink. Only problem was it never came open before! Talk about the shit being scared out of you! I did a double take, the face was gone and I sure wasn't going to wait and see where the body was!

I ran out the door so fast I looked like the official roadrunner! Only problem was I had nowhere to go! It was almost eleven o'clock at night and I remembered my mom was still at work. I just wanted to talk to her. I knew she would tell me it was my imagination but,

I was prepared to let her know my imagination just shit all the way down the street!

Lucky for me I had a quarter in my pocket so I called her. She never learned to drive so I knew her ride would not want to listen to my chanting. So I just told her what happened! I didn't expect anything from her I just needed to clear my head and hear her voice.

I finally went back to my apartment after carefully looking around. I climbed up and shut the closet door and as long as I lived there the door never came open again!

THE NIGHTMARE

It was morning I had survived the night sorta. Actually I had had a nightmare. I guess I couldn't get it through my head what Eunice was trying to tell me. I could see a watch of some kind but assumed he was telling me something about the timing not being right. You know like his death was not at the right time it wasn't his rightful time to go kinda thing. Or maybe he was telling me his watch was missing or something. Maybe he wanted me to look for the watch and give it to someone.

Anyway, after the events of the night I was still a little unnerved, well, come on, tell me you would have stayed in the apartment, where the body was coming after the head!

I finally feel asleep toward the wee hours of the morning. When I finally slept it was not without a horrible nightmare. I could see my dad. His eyes were wild looking like he had gone mad or something. He had a shovel in his right hand and was going along side a mountain.

It had been raining and he was pulling me with the other hand. I was shocked to see myself donned in a beautiful wedding gown! I was trying to get away from him but the harder I struggled the stronger he became. It was raining harder now and the muddy ground where he had been digging was like quick sand and really hard to keep standing.

The crack of lighting lit up the sky giving light to what was a very dark night on the side of the mountain. Somehow I knew we were in West Virginia on the cliff overlooking the old home place. I don't know why he chose that place in my dream as there really was a cemetery in the yard. It would certainly have been easier to dig up whatever was lying there or wherever he planned on burying!

My dress was all muddy as I slipped into the mud, he still had a firm grasp on my arm. "What are you doing" I shouted! He turned to me and said "You should have married him! It's time!"

I screamed "He's dead!" I suddenly knew what he was doing, it was not who he was going to dig up. It was whom he was going to bury! I woke up sweating and out of breath, but alive and safe in own apartment, my own bed! It was just a nightmare! Or, was it!

I was at work when my mom called and said my dad had been so depressed after his friends funeral. Truthfully I wasn't all that great myself, as I was the one my dad called that morning when he found his friend dead on the kitchen floor!

My mom was in Ohio visiting my brother and I was at work. The two of them had been on a long week-end of drinking everything in sight and using prescription drugs. It really shouldn't have been a surprise to find one or both of them dead at one point.

He never called me for anything, he was beside himself with grief and torment. I could hear it in his voice. I came as quickly as I could. My younger sister Raynee had just arrived, just as surprised as I was that we were the ones he called. His dead body still dead on the floor, the cops were there and the coroner had just entered. No wonder I had night mares! It was just awful after that.

During the funeral you could tell he was barely holding it together. He was devastated and he wasn't the only one as he grabbed my hand at the funeral home and made me touch his cold dead face! He told me it was a way of forgetting him!

What the hell kind of sense did that make! It's probably what triggered his face in the mirror and the door popping open not to mention the whole nightmare thing! Besides he was "His" friend!

Plus he probably scarred me for life or prepared me in a morbid way to my destiny.

A few days later my mom called and asked me to ride with her and my brother-in-law to West Virginia. My dad wanted to just get away for awhile. I was a little hesitant as I never got along with my dad anyway and after the nightmare, well yikes!

I knew my mom wanted me to go so I agreed. They picked me up from work and stopped by my apartment to get my clothes. My mom came in with me and I told her of my dream.

Once back in the car we were on our way. My dad had a station wagon, nine passenger so the back seats laid down nicely. He being so depressed decided to sleep the entire trip. He had not spoken a word for miles. All of a sudden he sat up in the back leaning over the seat and said "It was time, you should have married him."

I turned to look at him, his eyes were wild and crazy looking. He turned and laid back down as though he had not spoken a word! My mom looked at me in disbelief, we had no words to be spoken.

You can bet that when we arrived I carried the suitcases in myself, and looked for a shovel and a wedding dress! His friend always liked me but believe me there was no way I would have ever married him! He was older than my dad for starters, he smoked a cigar, drank to much and was virtually a slob!

However he had a good heart and was my dad's best friend. He would do anything for any of us. I later learned what he had been trying to tell me. He had had a very expensive wrist watch that mysteriously came up missing after the police and coroner had left that day. I think he wanted my dad to have it.

However, with no proof I was unable to help. I think he was satisfied just knowing that I finally knew what he was trying to tell me. I never saw his face again after that. The healing process and the guilt my dad had to live with lasted his life time. So sad for him, thinking and blaming himself and missing his friend, never really knowing if he could have saved him. But the drinking continued drowning the guilt. Ironically the thing he blamed himself for, being to out of it to hear the last cries for help was the only way he could go on.

When my dad passed in 1987, he was buried in West Virginia. Craziest thing was he was not buried in the old cemetery just outside the house. He was buried on the cliff, where he dragged me for my wedding burial that muddy, rainy night in my nightmare so long ago!

I remember how I felt as we went up the mountain, the nightmare ever so clear in my head. They sat the coffin down and I stood there starring at it. I don't remember any words that were said or memories that were shared. I turned as we left him alone, a single grave high on the cliff, overlooking the home place where I was born.

I remember his last breath. I had told him earlier that mom was on her way. They had separated several years before, she was living in California, it would take time for her to arrive and I wasn't sure she was coming. I had never really gotten along with my dad, but I had never lied to him. It just made me feel worse, to give him false hope.

He laid there for hours, suffering then slipped into a semi coma. They all held hands as they stood around his bed. I stood alone at the foot. He was almost gone, the breathing had almost stopped.

All of a sudden he opened his eyes, looked desperately around the group. He seemed almost frantic, trying to find someone. I thought he was looking for my mom. Through it all he still loved her. I felt sorry for him as she wasn't there. He wouldn't get to see her before he would go!

His eyes met mine, stopped and he focused on me. He smiled at me, pointed to me and gave me a wink, then he was gone! It was as if he finally understood me in a strange sort of way. It was just to odd that I would be the last one he would ever see! Me, the one he feared it seemed at times. Me the one he tried to kill. Me the one he liked the least. What truth did he uncover at deaths door, and what did I have to do with it!?

All those thoughts rambled through my head, it was a lot to think about. Did he see someone beside me, behind me or was it me. I shuddered at the irony of all that had taken place throughout my life.

Everyone was in the house by now going thru his things, I couldn't, it didn't feel right. I left the house and stood alone looking up at his final resting place. Floods of dark memories fell around me, then the light that shed the darkness gave me a sparkle of such few good memories.

I smiled as I promised myself I would hold onto them, after all my mom loved him, once upon a time. I realized he was a troubled soul, blaming himself for his brother's death and his friends death. Losing his family and never fully understanding why, or what he did that was so wrong. I think he did love us, as much as he knew how, maybe his void of emotion protected him some how.

I heard a bird singing in the distance, the soft wind caressed my face, I had been bitter to long, I knew I could never forget no matter how hard I would try, but I could do something for him.

Long ago I swore he would never make me cry. I shed one last tear for him, as I forgave him. I looked up as the sun peeked thru the trees casting a shadow over his resting place. Somehow we were both set free, I knew it in my heart as I swallowed the lump in my throat, and wiped the tear from my eye.

I thought I saw a shadow dart into the nearby trees, and for a brief moment three knocks came from behind me. Then three more knocks, he seemed to look at me. The woodpecker sat silently for a moment, it was as though he wanted to make sure he had my attention. He then spread his wings and flew across the sky. I watched his carefree flight, he swooped down across my dad's final resting place then into the trees and disappeared.

Was it a sign that he was finally free? I closed my eyes and prayed he had found peace, joined with his family and friends, but mostly I prayed all his torments were gone.

INVISIBLE

I really honestly don't believe this ever happened. Everyone says it happened and they have no reason to lie, yet I have no memory of where I went. So typically wouldn't that mean it didn't happen! Is it a memory like so many hidden in the depths of my mind that is waiting to yet be revealed. Perhaps locked deep inside, until the information is needed. If so, what does it mean? Better yet would I understand it? "Do I really want to?"

The day started out like any normal day, except for the fact it was storming outside. It was a Friday I was cleaning my small apartment. My brother and his family were coming for the weekend. I hadn't seen them in awhile and they hadn't yet seen the newest member of our family. My sister's beautiful baby daughter. It would be nice to see the little cousins reaction to each other.

We lived in the same apartment above the strand theatre. The very same one of my dreams and the man in the mirror. Nothing had happened for a while and the rent was cheap, that's why we stayed.

Everything was clean and ready for their arrival. My Mom had stopped in for a little while before she went to work saying she would see everyone when she got off. A little while later they arrived.

We sat and talked for awhile. I made dinner and after we put the kids down for the night we played cards. The storm gained momentum as a loud burst of thunder seemed to shake the entire building. We started laughing as my brother had just taken a big gulp of his soda at the same time as the thunder, spitting it all over himself!

The electric blinked a few times warning it could go out at any given moment. I started searching for candles. A few minutes later, we were in the dark! We sat there for a few minutes. The flashing of the lighting was wicked and fast, large rain drops hitting hard against the window. Another burst of thunder sent chills down my back. Sirens could be heard from the street below, I felt sorry for the ones who had to be out on a night like tonight.

The babies remained quiet, although I don't know how they were able to sleep thru it. I had to find a candle or flashlight soon, it would be a matter of time before the babies would wake. I felt my way into the darkness and searched the drawer for a flashlight or candles. Finally, a candle! I started back thru to the others when a knock came from the door.

My brother lit the candle and I answered the door. It was my boyfriend, a deputy sheriff, drenched from head to toe! He was still on duty but had a few minutes. He wanted to drop in and make sure we were okay since there was no electricity for several blocks.

He left a little while later, we sat staring at the candlelight. The flickering of the light left an eerie glow making shadows on the walls. We started telling "Ghost Stories". Only made up ones of course, with the exception of the apartment we lived in together in Ohio.

We started talking about the crazy landlady, the storm, and of course the hanging man! We talked about the dreams each of us had had that night, and the strange words I spoke when they awakened me. My hand and fingers in the air touching the plaque no one else saw, as I recited the words. "Lead me teach me to where there is no wrong".

We recalled and relived the dream when we reached my mom's apartment. We remember how we felt and each step we took being identical to my description in the dream. The long dark hallway. The rubber like stairs, the bathroom on the left and down the hall from my mom's apartment. Every detail so exact, and yet I nor them had ever been there until the three of us that day.

It would have been the perfect time to spill my guts and further discuss the strange encounters throughout my years. Something in the back of my mind prevented me, it was like it was a secret meant only for me. It was as if I would tell, I would be breaking some kind of trust. A trust that goes deep within me, even though I didn't understand it. I knew whatever it was I somehow was special to it. I was never special to anyone before. I knew I didn't trust many people, and I wouldn't break that bond just yet.

When some of the pieces start to make some kind of crazy sense, then it could be revealed. I was still very guarded about revealing things that I didn't even believe myself, but, couldn't deny the fact that they did indeed happen! I tried to convince myself it was just my imagination when I was a kid. It's just to vivid, to real, I know what I saw, I knew what I heard and I know what I know and that's all I know. One thing I am absolutely positive of "I do not understand, I do not understand why, I do not understand any of it! Notta, nothing, ziltch, zero!"

It was just after midnight when another knock came at the door, we thought it was my mother. When I opened the door there was no one. The long dark hallway was even darker, with no windows for a chance of lighting to brighten it up. I stepped into the hall with the candle. Shadows seemed to jump along the hall with the flickering of the flame.

I turned to the others "You heard that right?" they answered "Yes, it was most definitely a knock". I shrugged my shoulders, I told my brother it was time for mom, we better go down and wait for her. She would never be able to see in the dark. Her ride wouldn't want to block any traffic and I wouldn't want her standing in the rain.

We started down the hall when the lights came back on! "Yay"! I said. Just as we reached the downstairs door, she was getting out of the car. Perfect timing! We went back up talking quietly as we didn't want to awaken the old man that lived across the hall from us and of course the landlady who lived in the very front apartment.

We visited for a while longer and the storm quieted down. My brother took my mom home and came back a little while later. It was almost 2am when my sister's baby woke for her bottle. My sisters apartment was down the hall and I agreed to get her bottle.

I couldn't help but glance toward the bathroom every time I walked the hall. The lady still fresh in my mind. The dream always came back no matter how hard I tried to dismiss it. It was especially so tonight, as we had bought up the whole thing again! I hoped we didn't awaken the evil by talking about it! I hoped I wouldn't have another encounter with her, the man or the plaque!

After all it was only a dream! That was way to real, or perhaps it was not a dream at all but a glimpse into the future! Over the years I have had several that have come true, along with time lapses and events that I thought had already happened years before they actually did! Really messes with my head when those things happen. It's hard to bring myself to believe they just took place. Trying to convince others it was along time ago, they just look at me like I'm stupid or something!

Anyway, coast was clear, no one lurking that I could see anyway. I quietly ran down the hall and entered the apartment. Her apartment was very small, it was more like a room actually. She had a bed and a small refrigerator in the same room. Of course the bathroom was closer to her room than it was mine, but that was the only up side of it.

She didn't really stay in it much, mostly she was at my apartment. The only reason she got the apartment was because her husband was in the army. He was stationed in Germany and would be coming home on furlough soon.

I remember the room smelt somewhat musty, but given the rain and being shut up plus the oldness of the building, it wasn't unusual. I really had no need to turn the lights on, the street light outside and the light from the fridge was sufficient.

I was only gone a few minutes, so I was surprised when my brother came into the room and opened the fridge. He pulled out a second bottle, I was confused since the babies had different formulas. I said "I have her bottle", he acted as though I weren't there. "Hey, I have her bottle" I said again as I touched his shoulder. He never turned to look at me, I called his name, again it was like he never seen or heard me.

I followed him down the hall, thinking well maybe something happened to their baby's bottle. He opened the door and shut it in my face!

I opened the door "Gee thanks for shutting the door in my face!". I said, "I have her bottle." I started to hand it to my sister. Who sat there staring at me and feeding the baby with the bottle my brother had given her. Where have you been, they all seemed to ask at the same time. I was confused, "What do you mean?" "I told you I would get her bottle, and that's what I did."

"You've been gone for hours!" "She's had several bottles since then." Was the reply, as they looked at me in question. "Joe was here looking for you, we didn't know where you went!"

I laughed "Okay, I went down the hall, you saw me" I said looking at my brother. "I didn't know why you came to get her bottle." I saw you open the fridge, I spoke to you." "I told you I had it, but you ignored me." "See the bottle is still cold!" They looked at me, I thought they were just messing with me.

"I went to get her a bottle because you never came back!" He argued. I was dumbfounded. It wasn't funny anymore. "But, I saw you, you didn't turn the light on, you opened the fridge, I spoke to you, you looked at me, I touched your shoulder, you ignored me." "I don't know why your mad at me."

I walked with you down the hall. "You didn't need to shut the door in my face!"

"I don't know where you were, but, you weren't there". They were all looking at me. I just stood there. They didn't seem to be fooling around. It's not like my brother or my sister to ignore someone when they are mad. They usually confront them! I really don't know what happened, if anything did.

One thing is certain, I lost time somewhere, that night. I was as confused as they, as I looked out the window, at the sun shining. All traces of last night's storm was now gone, leaving me wondering and confused.

I thought of the other times in my life when I have lost time, leaving no memory of time captured or lost. We had never spoke of it after that night, many years ago. His kids now all grown, I didn't even know if he would remember. I had to know, I called my brother and asked him, making him swear he would tell me the truth. I thought now if he doesn't remember, then he was just messing with me.

He remembered so clearly, saying "You were gone for hours!" "If you had been in the apartment I would have seen you." "The place was way to small to have missed you, I called your name when I opened the door." I thought something had happened to you, I looked for you down the hall and outside." "You were gone".

My sisters story was the same. She didn't recall how long I was actually gone, but agreed it was several hours! "You were gone". The words rang out in my head. What seemed a few minutes to me was several hours to them. My brother didn't seem to see me. I at that time slipped into some kind of "Twilight Zone," another dimension.

I for that few minutes or several hours was a ghost, not able to reach the living! My words unheard, my touch unfelt. I can't help but wonder if the old woman, the man or the plaque was involved in any way. Taking me to continue what was started as a dream. What ever happened, unless my siblings were playing a trick that continues to this day. I was for that period of time "INVISIBLE"!

BLOODSTONE

Several years had gone by and little thoughts if any remained of the plaque. However the words still haunted me. There has to be more to it, a deeper meaning, but what was it?

By this time I had moved back to Ohio to start over again. All the things that I had endured when I lived here before were just memories. I had a new job a nice apartment and had met a wonderful man.

The future was looking up for me and I was the happiest I had ever been! The weekends were very special as that's when he would come to see me. He only lived an hour and half away but seemed so far away between visits. I had no phone so we were limited on communication. My brother had asked me just that evening, "What would I do if he popped the question?"

I just laughed, but wondered what the two of them discussed, since my brother did have a phone and they talked more than I did! I had only known him a few months and actually seen him a total of four times. It seemed very unlikely he would ask that question so soon. None the less it was indeed a case of love at first sight.

He really knew nothing of my past, and I knew nothing about his. The future after all was really all that mattered wasn't it? Besides if he knew how crazy my life had been he probably would have ran!

As it turned out that weekend he did propose to me! On the balcony of my brothers house, overlooking the neighborhood. It was cold and had been snowing but the moon was full and the night was magical.

He pulled a paper cigar ring out of his pocket, and I just laughed never saying yes and never saying no. it was the third ring he had given me in our short relationship. The first was the night we met. He took his ring off when my brother and my dad were having a discussion with several guys over a game of pool. He was my knight in shining armor and had came to my rescue! After the incident and everyone had calmed down he closed my hand over the ring and said keep it. I'll come for it, a little insurance that I will see you again! The third was a Christmas gift. A birthstone ring given to me the day after we met. The next weekend he bought a diamond ring and the rest is history. Hence making that ring number four! Three's a charm, right!? So actually it was three his was given back the day he came to see me.

He went back home and I stayed in Ohio, no plans were discussed. A lot had to be taken care of and we both needed to work.

Things had been fairly calm in the aspect of the crazy things my life was made up of. A few little unexplained things happened from time to time. I was I guess at that time at peace with the world of the paranormal. I had grown a lot and wasn't as confused when things did happen. I looked for causes when I couldn't find them I just accepted them. I knew if things continued I would definitely have to risk my happiness for the truth. I couldn't and wouldn't live a lie. I would warn him of the things in my life that were just crazy. It would be some kind of test I guess, if he stayed then we were meant to be. If he ran I wouldn't blame him.

Just when I thought things were quiet, a piece of my past was revealed. Something I had forgotten about. It was all innocent enough and started with a simple conversation with a stranger.

It was a Saturday afternoon. My brother and his wife had asked if I would care for the girls while they did some shopping and enjoyed a movie. I loved being with the kids so it was a pleasure. They were just babies a year old and a two year old. The fun stages, we played and I fed them lunch and later ice cream in the old antique rocker I had bought years earlier for story time. Even though they were very young they would cuddle on my lap with a blanket and listen to the stories and of course eat ice cream! It was a ritual with us, every time I came over that's what we did!

Just as I was getting them ready for our story time a knock came at the door. A girl my age stood on the porch. I smiled and said "Can I help you?" She asked about my brother and sister-in-law. Said she was a friend and had just gotten in town and wanted to see them. The girls seemed to know her so I invited her in out of the cold.

She introduced herself as Carol. I told her I was just about to put the girls down for a story and nap, and she was welcome to sit with us. Story time was over and two little bundles with ice cream mustaches were fast asleep. She helped me lay them down and we left the room closing the door slightly behind us.

I told her they should be back soon. I was always a little shy around people I didn't know so conversation wasn't my best quality. The television was on and just happened to be the near end of a scary movie. We sat in silence and watched the ending. It was then that she spoke. I was surprised to finally meet someone that had had a few things happen in her life that were to say the least on the crazy side. We struck up a conversation that was easy for us to relate to.

The subject of weird dreams came up. I decided to share one of mine with her as she had shared one with me. I began telling her about the dream I had had while living with my brother. I confided to her that all my life I had had strange things happen. I started talking about waking up and holding my hand and fingers as if they were on some kind of plaque, and chanting the words inscribed on it. When I described the plaque and told her I knew it had to mean something. Her eyes widened with interest. I spoke the words that had been so real then and just as real now. The words that had haunted me throughout my life, only to bring horror to her face!

She stood up and backed away from me. The hairs stood up on her arms. She started chanting, sentence after sentence spewed from her mouth. It was like a ritual prayer, something out of a horror movie of some kind. It was clearly some sort of occult prayer, worshipping the dark side! It was not possible I told myself, how could I have dreamed such a thing! Did I die and go to hell for a brief moment! What the crap man, this could not be what it most certainly is! The meaning of it, the source of its origin! It was creepy! She repeated it so fast I don't know what all she said. I was dumb founded, I had no words, I sat there when she was finished looking at her.

She had exhausted herself, her eyes were wide with concern and fear. What she had ran away from was now right in her face. Even though I sure didn't understand any of it, it had joined us in this crazy way. Was it to remind her she would never be free from it? Or was it to give me a little more of the puzzle and leave me wondering "What had happened, and where I was exposed, and most importantly "Why"!

Dead silence fell around us when she was finished. When I finally found my voice, I started asking questions. What and where and how did she know the rest of the prayer? Most importantly how did I come in contact with such a thing!

She told me a few years ago she had moved to California. She had gotten into some stuff and had joined an occult. The prayer was their prayer, one they recited upon every meeting. The group was called "SATANS DAUGHTERS"!

Whooo now! I had never been to California at that time, and certainly never had been in contact with any one that was mixed up in anything such as that! Heck, no one even knew the things that had happened in my life.

She came over to me and held my hands in hers. Her hands were cold and shaking. The prayer had somehow connected us as sisters, in that period of time. We held a bond, a secret so deep we knew it must be kept a secret! Our eyes meet. I saw terror in her eyes, then my own reflection, staring back at me. She spoke quietly trying to help me discover myself. Suddenly I saw it! Something shiny swinging back and forth in front of my eyes! About the same time she asked if I had in my possession a Blood Stone.

That was it! It all came back to me! I could see it clearly now the stone, the chain, swinging ever so gently back and forth in front of me. It was so clear I reached out to touch it, to stop it, but it was to late!

I realized after all those years I had after all been hypnotized! It wasn't impossible after all, even an unwilling recipient could and was under the influence! But why!? And how could he!

I began thinking back, things had happened all my life, maybe Busters mother had something to do with it. I remembered her placing her hand on my head that night and chanting something I didn't understand.

I remembered the devil doll and it trying to get me. Its claw scratching wildly behind the seat of the old Chevy pick-up. I remembered seeing the devil dancing in our dining room. Was it then that my soul belonged to him?

Then the obvious, my brother-in-law. It was hard to think he was capable of such a thing. Had he been in something far greater than he even understood!? Did he open a doorway without knowing? Was he in something beyond the playing around with hypnosis? Was he himself a bargaining tool for the dark knight? Did he have to sacrifice a soul in order to gain his back? What had he done!?

I had to know for myself. I would make the trip to their home when my fiancé came. I would insist on seeing the stone. I would remember, as it was so clear to me now. I had a lot to think about and even though the words haunted me throughout my life. I was somewhat grateful to at last know where it came from.

Later that day my fiancé arrived. I told him I needed to go to my sister's house. It was snowing and very cold out and she lived about a half hour away. He had no problem with it even though he had already driven a long way in the elements. I wanted to tell him why, but a part of me was still at an unrest with what I had just learned. Maybe after I see the stone, clarify for myself, make some sense of it. Then maybe I can come to a reasonable explanation. After all it had to be just a coincidence, a chance meeting, a dream. Maybe I was still dreaming, I could only hope!

We arrived about 8 o'clock, her two daughters ran to us as soon as we entered the room. We played with them for a little while and settled them in front of the television. My sister and I headed for the kitchen for bedtime snacks while the guys sat and talked about what guys talk about. I wasn't sure how I was going to bring up the subject of the bloodstone without to many questions. I would have to think of something.

Finally the opportunity came I told her I was going to buy a necklace and I happened to remember she had one like the one I wanted. I told her I thought it was called a bloodstone or something like that. Then did she still have hers and could I see it?

I followed her into the bedroom she picked up a key and inserted it into a jewelry box. Several necklaces, a watch, earrings, rings and a bracelet all neatly placed but no bloodstone. Before I could say anything she turned the jewelry box around and inserted another key in a hidden compartment.

There it was! All alone and hidden away, as if it held secrets and needed to be locked away for safe keeping. Was there another reason it was so secure and hidden from site. Did it hold memories for her as well. I reached in and held it in my hand. I looked at the stone I could once again see it swinging back and forth. There was no mistaking it, it was the same stone. Its beauty now turned ugly as I looked at it and suddenly remembered something that finally made sense!

The stone had been used before! I could see what had happened to my sister several years ago. Early in her marriage, it all made sense and I detested the man that had harmed her. Is that why the stone was locked away by itself? Was she hiding it from him? Did she figure it out herself, when she peeked in on us that night he hypnotized me. We were in there for so long she said. Did she suspect he had done something that he shouldn't have. Maybe it triggered a memory, a memory of what he did to her.

Was the stone locked away that night? Was it possible, with everything in my life that while I was under hypnotic suggestion that something got in? Something that lay in waiting catching me at the moment where I was most venerable. Perhaps using him as a tool and me a pawn. Or did he plant or invite something dark in, on purpose or by accident.

She looked puzzled as I starred at the necklace. Even though the stone had been locked away, I felt the evil that had been hidden deep within its crystals escaped. Its vial, although invisible once again surrounded me. Smothering me with the sickening reality of the truth as my innocence was taken by an unseen presence. My soul was no longer mine, stolen in that brief moment. I was now a lost soul and no one could help.

My heart sank as I held the stone, I opened my hand, looked at it again. How could something so beautiful and innocent, turn into something so dark and dangerous! I held it out to her, she seemed to be in deep thought herself. She surprised me by backing away when I tried to give it to her.

Did she remember, after all? I said nothing as I placed the stone back in the hidden compartment. I closed the drawer, drowning out the echo in my head. She carefully locked it and put the key in a nearby closet on the top shelf away from the jewelry box. I said nothing as I knew she wanted it as far away as she could put it. She didn't want to touch it, perhaps for fear of a memory now faded coming to haunt her.

On the way home my thoughts traveled backwards in time. To a time when my sister was first dating him. I remembered feeling sad when she left to finish her high school year and graduation, in another town. It meant I wouldn't get to see her much. I feared for some odd reason that I would never see her again. My older sister had already married and moved away but I could stay with her and her family from time to time. This just seemed different to me, he was somewhat a stranger, I guess and he took her away so soon.

I recall after they were married they had moved and no one knew where they were. It was like they just disappeared, it had been months, then when we did find her, she had changed. What did I know I was just in jr high, I didn't really understand what all was going on.

She sat in the king size bed, Indian style. Her hair hadn't been combed probably for a few days. She searched wildly scanning the entire room as though she were looking for some kind of recognition.

She wasn't my sister anymore, I didn't know her. Everyone said she had had a breakdown of some kind. But it was more than that. Now holding the stone and her resistance to take it back, I realized how powerful the stone had become in the wrong hands. It was like I could see its crystals like a mirror revealing a dark past and once again innocence had died. What had he done!?

You see, she was somebody else, even down to her name. She didn't know me, and yet she did. Her head was so messed up. When she did speak, it was a whisper. I was shocked when she told me she was dead! Then she said her name was Marnie. She rocked back and forth and giggled a little then grabbed my hand. Her wild eyes met mine and she whispered in my ear, "but you can see me can't you?" When he would come into the room she would pull the covers up, only her eyes were visible. She was afraid.

It was a little while before she was finally herself. Now that I think about it, as messed up as she was, it should have taken a lot more time than that. Perhaps, he decided he best fix what he had done and maybe that's why she was herself again. Maybe he was afraid his antics would be discovered!

I remember afterwards no one spoke of it, it was like it never happened. She didn't remember it and it was best left alone. Besides in my wildest imagination I would never have suspected he had done that to her. Now after all those years the truth has surfaced.

I recalled a re-occurring dream or nightmare she had had. She confided in me on several different occasions. It bothered her and frightened her as well. She couldn't escape the fact it was so clear, it was always the same. Every detail of the dream was just as she told me the first time. I often thought due to the contents it was perhaps a conjuring of her mixed up emotions bottled up in a suggestion of

137

some sort. Of course I didn't realize it at the time, but I have my suspicions that the bloodstone was involved!

She was in a huge old mansion. The halls were dark lit only by sconces containing candles. The little bit of light they produced danced along the long dingy, depressing hallways. She walked the halls peering in open doorways, each room the same, sparsely lit with candles and the flickering of a fireplace here and there. She could hear wailing coming from somewhere. She said it was a sound of desperation, and sadness. It was so overwhelming It sent chills thru her body all the way to her soul! Each step she took the wailing grew louder.

The winding dark staircase seemed to go on with no ending. Finally she came to a heavily locked door, just off the landing. The wailing continued, she called out to the person locked inside. The wailing softened, and grew to a forlorn whimpering, like her heart and soul had been ripped to nothing. She looked desperately for a key, none was in sight. She found a nearby chair and pulled it to the door standing on the seat she searched the top of the door frame for a key. No luck. She moved the chair away from the door and there on the floor was a large key ring. It reminded her of an old scary movie. The ring itself was made of a heavy cast iron, at least fifty keys hung from the ring. Funny it wasn't there before.

She tried key after key, until the lock popped open. She slowly opened the door, she spoke in a soft voice to the whimpering spirit broken woman. The woman stood in the corner of the room, her back turned away from my sister. My sister cautiously walked over to the woman speaking softly, trying to comfort the woman. The whimpering stopped as my sister touched her shoulder. The woman turned to face her.

A look of horror comes across my sister's face. She backs away, freezes then screams in horror as she is face to face with none other than herself!

Then there is my younger sister, still haunted to this day of a man, dark, tall wearing a hat and trench coat always watching. Then the night she swore the devil had been in her room! She had never been tortured by anything until then. Did he plant that into her head that night as well?

Did he innocently stumble into something dark when he was experimenting with hypnotic suggestions. Or was something dark lurking and waiting for a chance to enter this realm. Did he call unto something dark then realize he had gone to far? Did he then bargain and trade or give away innocent souls to spare himself from what he had created.

There was a lot for me to think about. I couldn't remember the rest of the chant that had been inscribed on the plaque. I still don't know at what cost my final payment will be. I don't know where I went that night under deeper hypnoses than I knew. Neither do I know what I undertook in that dark place so many years ago. Could I be held accountable for something I did under someone's influence?

I looked up into the sky and silently asked God to forgive me for whatever I did. When I opened my eyes I couldn't shake the doom that seemed to surround me. There doesn't seem to be a way out. I can feel it, it waits silently, like a creature in the night. Forever stalking, lurking around every corner waiting!

Haunting me forever!

ROBERT RETURNS

Funny how things are more connected than we can imagine at the time. I always said everyone we meet in life there is a reason. Oh, we may not understand it at the time but it's there waiting for an unexpected reveal. Some people we meet simple are there to teach us life's valuable lessons. While others are a reminder of just how blessed we really are, for some things are not always what they appear to be.

Over the years we are subjected to people. We learn from them, their mistakes, their misfortunes, their happiness, their sorrow, their gentleness, kindness compassion. Their hidden secrets their vengeance, their torments, their greed, and sometimes how violent a person can become. We are made aware of all human aspects and behaviors to protect ourselves. Everyone is unique in their own way and we learn from each of them everyday. Some lessons are hard and we are made to face the reality of what we choose to learn from others.

Sometimes we meet to bring our past back to us and unite us in the strangest ways. The why's are what we don't really comprehend. It's like a piece of the puzzle of our very being that becomes questionable. Sometimes we are forced to accept the fact that there is another part of us. Perhaps one that we have already experienced that we somehow must find again. Perhaps in another life we have buried in the backs of our minds and a piece sometimes surfaces to give us a hint to the full understanding of our lives.

When I left Indiana it was like a breath of fresh air. A whole new world had emerged right before my eyes. I vowed never to return the place that I often referred to as hell's "hot spot". But as fate would have it we returned in March of 1979. My husband had became ill and his family wanted us closer. It was a very hard thing for me with the news of his illness and his longing to be near his family.

So, it was my love for him that I agreed to come back to the gates of a hell. I tried to tell myself it was for the best and it would be different.

My oldest son was 2 and a half and my youngest son was 8months old when they first met their grandparents. I had only met them once prior to that myself so they knew very little about me.

My father in-law was a janitor at my old elementary school. My husband had also worked there when we first met. But since we had only known each other four days prior to our getting married it was not anything that we really discussed. Let me back up a minute, we met December the 23, and were married March 3. But, I say we only knew each other four days because I lived in Dayton, Ohio and I only saw him four times before we were married. Sounds crazy I know, but, when you know you know!

It was definitely love at first sight, and we had planned on starting our new lives together in California, nothing else mattered!

Anyway we were at my in-laws home one evening when my father in-law came home carrying a box full of toys. He sat them down in the middle of the room and said the boys could each pick out one toy. He had gotten them from the school, they were old and the kids hadn't played with them for quite some time.

My oldest son started going thru the box and soon picked out his treasure. My youngest son was barely walking at the time soon followed. He pulled out toys and tossed them all over the floor.

My heart stopped when he pulled out the all so familiar "My Robert". I couldn't believe my eyes! He had survived all those years and looked the same as he had so long ago! His painted turned up mouth smiled at me when our eyes met. I was in shock, I couldn't believe "My Robert" had came back to me in such an unsuspecting way!

I wanted to jump out of my seat and grab him and hug him! I sat still instead trying to keep my emotions in tack. I couldn't let them know about Robert it was to personal and for him to have waited all these years to come back to me. The chances were just to slim and I hadn't thought about him for many years.

Imagine my surprise when my son, my little baby, picked him up and carried him over to me and laid him in my lap! He smiled at me as if he knew how much the doll meant to me. I picked him up and hugged him. All those memories of a childhood long ago flooded through me. I was home, and so after twenty two years of him waiting he also was finally home!

We experienced all kinds of things after Robert came to live with us. But, I never blamed him for any of it. Fact was I had had so many bazaar things that had taken place in my life over the years that I certainly didn't blame him for. Then again, maybe that was just the opening other entities needed to burst into this world and invade mine!

Any way over the years we made a decision to move to the country. We moved a little at a time and one night our house was broken into. We didn't have a lot to retrieve at the time, however the thing we didn't yet move was very important to me.

It was my trunk with my special things inside and my precious "Robert" was gone! I was heart sick. He had been thru so much and so many years trying to reconnect with me and now he was lost!

I suspected the neighbors kids as they were very unruly and always in some kind of trouble. I just couldn't prove it, that was the problem. I imagined what hell they would put my Robert through as they were also known for destroying things. I felt so sad that I had not taken better care to protect my Robert. I only hoped he would find his way back as he had so many years ago.

I waited patiently for a long time and finally had to accept the fact that he had met his fate at the hands of those horrible children. Little did I realize he would find me again in the most unusual way and in a place where I would never have dreamed I'd be, so many years later!

ROBERT

I had a lot to think about from my first encounter with Robert. I was so caught up in him. He was certainly capable of doing things. I remembered when we were moving into the house in the country, we were so busy taking loads over from one house to the other. The trunk that I placed Robert in as well as a few other precious things to me were to be picked up on our final load. It was a very sad thing for me to find our house had been robbed and my trunk was now gone along with other pieces of household goods. I was certain who had taken it but, with no proof the police couldn't do anything and the parents of the thieves were no help! I was so angry at myself for not taking the trunk first!

Was Robert really gone, or was he angry at being left behind!? After all he had came back to me after many years. Was he in fact the starting of my crazy life, is that why he came back? Was he here to protect me? When I think back nothing paranormal in any way with the exception of my Grandfathers passing and final visit had happened, during our time in California. We hadn't been back to hell very long before Robert came back into our lives.

I remember being so happy to see him again! I couldn't get over the fact he was so untarnished through the years. I looked into his eyes and that turned up painted smile. Over the years he should have shown some wear. It made me sad to think he had perhaps been left alone on the bottom shelf where I said good-bye to him. All those years I was busy growing up, he lay there waiting for my return.

I held him close to me as I remembered some of my happiest times, always excited to go to school and be with my friend. A smile escaped my lips as I wondered how Miss Selvey really felt about my Robert. I think back and I can see her face. She didn't smile much at me as I recall. I can remember how nervous she was when she had put him high on the shelf, to only find him next to me a short time later.

She must have seen the signs, she had to know it wasn't normal. Maybe she was afraid to say anything lest people think she was crazy. Whatever the reason, it was clear my Robert had remained untouched throughout the years. Of course, as I think about him, he was a very old doll when I was a child. Was he indestructible? Or sadly very alone without me? Had he known we would be together again? We had a very strange bond, of course being a child it was not something I thought about. I was just so happy he was with me again.

My life was crazy and from time to time I could just look at my Robert and hug him, taking myself back to a simpler time. Somewhere in my fading memories sparks of feeling comfort when I was sad, he was always there for me. Now he was back. The little girl inside me wanted to curl up beside him and tell him my troubles. I just needed him to tell me everything would be okay. I needed him to take care of me just as he did a life time ago. It was as though he knew I would need him. Is that why he came back, is that how he found me?

Good grief! What am I saying! He's a doll and I'm not that lonely little girl anymore! Although, I have to admit he always takes me to that safe place in my mind. I told myself the fact that after all those years we found each other, it after all, had to mean something! I mean really what were the odds that anything this bizarre could ever happen! Why would our paths meet again if there wasn't a purpose!?

I felt as though my life were falling apart. My husband was very ill and spent a lot of time in the hospital an hour and a half away. My precious little boys couldn't possibly understand what was happening. I spent many hours away from them. I was needed at the hospital leaving them with their grandparents, which they barely knew. I shed no tears on the outside, after all I had to remain strong even though my life was falling apart.

We tried giving our boys a normal life, God knows I never had one! We played games with them read stories, watched movies as well as done crafts and paintings. I would take them bike riding one on the back seat of my bike and the other on the bar in front of me. It became our only transportation at the time, since I didn't yet have a license.

Time marches on and my husband would have good days as well as bad. In and out of the hospital. It was just our life, always on the edge.

Things had started to happen again. The knocks on the bedroom doors, Items coming up missing. Cold spots, hot spots. Feelings of constantly being watched. Shadows and that dam radio! I thought I would lose my mind! I would wake my husband in the middle of the night pleading with him to please make the radio stop! It was all jumbled, in between stations static that wouldn't stop! He would just smile and give me a hug saying there was no radio, no noise. Why couldn't he hear it!? Was I after everything I had been through now losing my mind when I needed it the most!

I just didn't have time for anymore disruptions it was all I could handle. I tried ignoring anything that just wasn't normal. The kids and I were the ones affected, it just didn't make sense that he couldn't hear the footsteps and the knocking! His medication had altered his eye sight for awhile, so that would explain him not seeing the shadows. I would distract the children when the noises would start, I would tell them it was a woodpecker or whatever I could think of at the time. I didn't want my children to be afraid.

I had made friends with a neighbor and when my husband was in the hospital we spent a lot of time together. She was recently divorced and had three children. Her son was my oldest sons age and they got along so well. We watched out for each other. Her ex was giving her a really bad time, sneaking around trying to make her life miserable. He was a threat to her and her children and had told her he would kill her. She sometimes would stay at my house and I at hers.

Needless to say when things started happening Tina no longer came over, even in the daytime. One night I was home alone just getting the kids ready for bed when the phone rang." Please come over" She said "I have a feeling it's going to be a bad night."

We played with the kids and just hung out. The phone calls started, he was threatening her, arguing with her. I could tell she was really scared. I told her I had a gun and I would go get it. He would at least stop and think before he tried anything and we could hold him off until the police could come.

She insisted on going with me across the street in case he was already lurking about. It was well after midnight, the night air seemed thicker than usual. The closer we got to the front door the feeling that something was just not quite right hung over us. She refused to come in but stood at the door looking in. My parrot Captain Jinks stood on his perch not moving. I walked over to him to pet his head he never moved or acknowledged that I was there. I gently shook the cage, he never moved or made a sound. I called his name and tried to give him a peanut. He sat there staring.

I felt heaviness all around and I hurried to my room which was off the kitchen to grab my shotgun. I was alarmed when it was NOT THERE! I yelled for her to help me find it. She refused to come in "Hurry." She pleaded. Her voice was growing to almost a frantic note. I was confused, my gun was always within reach! Now it was nowhere to be seen! I had a waterbed so it could not have gotten under the bed. It was simply gone! Loud noises and a growl came from somewhere near the back bedrooms. She screamed "Hurry! Come on, get out of there!"

I ran to the door saying "My gun is gone! I have to find it!" She opened the screen and grabbed my arm pulling me out the door. I reached in and slammed the front door shut as we ran back to her house.

We were on needles and pins as the children slept. I was worried about where my gun was and she was worried about her ex showing up. It was a long night. We had fallen asleep at some point, and the remainder of the night was thankfully uneventful.

I returned home when the sun came up, she kept the boys at her house and I started cleaning. I had to find my gun! The television was on in the living room and in my bedroom. Both were on the same station, I listened while I was cleaning. Funny thing happened, I called her to come and check it out. I knew she wouldn't come in, I assured her she could see it from the door.

She arrived a short time later, standing on the step peeking in. I asked her to look at both televisions which the way they were positioned she could see them. They were both on the same channel, however the sounds coming out were completely different! I changed the channels on both televisions to the same channel. Again the sounds were different! The television in the living room matched the program, the television in the bedroom was more of words trying to filter thru a mass of static! I then turned the television in the bedroom off and carried it into the kitchen at her request. I plugged it in, turned it on and it was the same as the living room sound and all!

Captain Jinks continued to act funny, he stayed in the corner of his cage facing the wall. I could not get him to move. He seemed to be in a trance or was to scared to move, I wasn't sure which. I patted his head trying to make him snap out of it, he ignored me. It was creepy to say the least.

Tina asked me if she could have her friend come over to meet me. She told me she was a Physic and swore she wouldn't tell her anything! I agreed, reminding her to pinky swear, on the bible that she would not tell her anything at all. This agreed on she was to come in a couple hours.

They arrived some time later. We were introduced, she told me to call her Bren. I excused myself mainly so she could get the feel of the house, without me in the room. I came back carrying drinks and a snack. She sat on the sofa with Tina next to her. I glanced at Tina, I knew she didn't want to come in but so far she was keeping it together. I noticed Bren was somewhat growing uneasy. I noticed her looking toward the back of the house. Then towards the kitchen.

Tina spoke for the first time, "Are you okay Bren?" She had known Bren for many years, she knew she had picked up on something. "It's okay, she already knows something is here." Bren looked at me I nodded my head and gave her permission to go thru the house.

I could tell she was apprehensive about it, but, nonetheless she headed for the kitchen area. We followed as she went towards my room. She stopped just outside the doorway. Then back to the back of the house. "I wouldn't want to be here at night." She said. "Oh, I don't mean to scare you, but you have something not good and not just one lurking here." "I'm sorry, I really need to get out of here."

They left a few minutes after that. Well that was just wonderful news to hear, I whispered to myself. "Super!"

They left and Bren told me I really shouldn't be there at night. I smiled and said "It's my home, it will be okay." She couldn't have known I had been plagued all my life with spirits. I really didn't feel the need to tell her. Besides she was after all physic, so she already knew, "Right?"

I finished cleaning, I was a little surprised to find my shotgun, just where it had always been! Within grasp right beside the bed! Strange I thought. Then I thought everything happens for a reason. Perhaps the gun went missing to protect us from maybe something bad that could have happened, had her husband showed up. I guess I will never know.

That night I bathed the kids and put them in my bed. She was right about one thing something indeed was lurking. Robert wasn't in his usual spot. I thought perhaps Bren had moved him on her tour of the house. It had been a long day, I showered and decided to read a little. I just started to nod off to sleep when a familiar sound echoed thru the house. I sat up abruptly when I heard the distinct sound of my rocking chair. I knew the perpetrator wanted me to know he was there. I had double checked the doors and windows, how could anyone have gotten in!?

I got out of bed and grabbed for my shotgun. I didn't want to leave the boys alone since my house was like a circle. You could go from the living room down the hall to one of the bedrooms, then thru a bathroom, to the laundry room and end up in the kitchen or in my bedroom. Leaving the boys would be risky.

I glanced around the room, something caught my eye. There he sat in the corner by the fireplace, my Robert! I quietly walked over and picked him up, I hugged him for reassurance and placed him beside my boys. Its bizarre to say the least but in my own way I knew he would watch over them like he had taken care of me. I quietly tiptoed over to the doorway. The rocker continued to rock.

My heart raced as I made a bold run to the living room gun aimed as I turned the corner revealing the rocker! THE EMPTY ROCKER!

I ran back to the boys, gun ready to fire. No sign of anyone. Loud footsteps echoed from the back bedroom. I ran to the bathroom a few feet away from my room and peeped into the bedroom. Alert and ready to face the intruder. My adrenaline was a record high! I was never more ready to fight than at that moment! My boys were my life and I would protect them!

Captain Jinks although I hit his cage as I ran through, never made a sound. It was as if he were in a trance. The house was suddenly quiet! I ran back to my boys and waited. I sat down on the corner of the bed. Watching the doorway. The house still dark, I suddenly snickered as I thought about all the horror movies I had seen over the years, and I would say out loud "Turn the lights on! "Yet there I sat in the darkness where there was electricity! Funny I thought they could certainly see me in the dark, maybe I should turn on the light! Maybe they couldn't see us with the light on! Yet, I still sat there. I could see with the help of the moonlight coming thru the kitchen window. I told myself I would see them before they would see me. A feeling came over me, it didn't seem to matter anymore.

Suddenly I laid the gun down on the floor up against the bed rail. I knew a gun would not protect us. I could feel it standing in front of me. It was so cold. I started shaking from the coldness that emanated from the thing that stood there. I looked at my boys, and Robert, his smile looking a little sinister in the dark. I wasn't afraid and I honestly don't know why. I looked into the face of the darkness. I knew there were more of them.

I felt surrounded, it was as if a circle had come together. I could hear whispers, feel movement. I could see shadows thru the moonlight. A skeletal figure could be seen by the doorway. My music box started playing. I sat down on the bed, I actually felt an unusual calmness come over me. I don't know if it was a sort of defeat or I felt brave with Robert once again in my life. I also knew even if I were afraid never show fear.

I looked at Robert, I was that helpless little girl again. I held him close to me, I picked up my bible laid it on my chest, I covered my boys with my other hand. It was all the protection I could give them. Bren's words echoed in my head "I wouldn't want to be here at night." Did she know what was coming?

Warmness filled the room and the coldness left as silently as it had entered. I laid down beside my children suddenly exhausted. I was thankful the children had slept thru it. I closed my eyes, I just wanted to sleep. A thought popped into my head and I sat up. I gently shook my oldest son and then my baby. I had to know even though they slept thru it all, that they were okay and untouched. I pulled them closer to me, I couldn't hold them close enough. Sleep finally came and the night turned into a beautiful day.

Everything seemed to quiet down for a few days. I saw no need in telling anyone what had taken place. My husband had been released from the hospital and he certainly didn't need to know. I had moved a hospital bed into the back bedroom. I moved all of us in there. Toys, kids everything. We only used the bedroom, kitchen and bathroom. I needed to keep my family as close and as safe as possible. I prayed the circle of darkness would not return. The boys were happy, Captain Jinks was back to his normal self my husband was home and I was on guard!

Tina and I were going to the grocery, I settled the kids in with coloring books and a cartoon. Although the children were to young to leave with my husband being bed bound, I had to go to the store. Her daughters were a phone call away and agreed to come running if needed. We wouldn't be gone long, phone at bedside, drinks and snacks they were good to go.

It was winter time and snow now covered the ground. We lived in a small town and there was a Grocery, a gas station and a post office. With any luck we would be able to get what we needed with out going to the next town. We weren't gone long, just as promised. I entered the house groceries in hand, announcing my arrival. I sat the groceries on the counter and headed for the bedroom to check on everyone before starting supper.

I was surprised to find my youngest son cradled in the arms of my husband, shaking and sobbing. My oldest son sat on the other side holding onto his brother's hand. I ran over to the bed. Looking puzzled. My husband spoke quietly to my son. "Tell mommy what happened."

Through tears and a shaky little voice he said, "Me was coloring and a peach alm weached round the door and gwabbed me!" My heart sank, I became angry. I had to hold it inside. I had been teaching him his colors and was proud that he could identify the color, just not the way it came about! I looked at my older son, he said "I had to pull him back in Mommy, but I didn't see it." I smiled at him and told him he was my brave little boy. I picked my baby up and held him close until he finally stopped sobbing. We started playing games and singing to take their minds off the horror I left them in.

The night was uneventful, I stayed alert the biggest part of the night holding my boys close. My husband in the hospital bed also alert I had finally told him of the events that had taken place. My husband really never fully believed in things he couldn't see. However, after he saw the terror on our son's face and I told him what had been happening, he believed! I laid Robert on the foot of the bed and my bible on my chest, arm over the boys. I was very angry, I had a lot on my mind. I finally drifted off to sleep.

The morning sun gaped thru the blinds announcing time to get up. My husband had a doctor appointment that afternoon. He would be gone for several hours. His father and brother were coming to take him as he would need their assistance. I asked Tina to care for my boys as I had a crow to pick! She agreed but made me promise to get out if things went badly. She just didn't know how badly things already were!

Once everyone was out of the house I set out to find where it was hiding. I slammed doors open hard enough to knock them down all the while calling it out! "You coward!" I screamed. "Show yourself!" I demanded as I busted through every room in the house, I taunted and demanded and yelled and screamed "You coward!" "Don't ever scare my kids again!" "Show yourself!"

All was quiet. Not a sound. No footsteps. No shadows. No coldness. No sign of an intruder. No evidence a presence had ever invaded at all! I stormed thru the house one last time, I recited the lords prayer and then "In the name of Jesus I rebuke thee!"

My eyes rested on Robert. I sat down and picked him up. I looked into his eyes, his turned up painted smile melted my heart. I recalled days long past and the havoc he caused. A thought occurred to me. Could Robert be responsible for the crazy things that are happening?

"Oh, Robert." I whispered. Then I just hugged him, and put the thought out of my head. There was no way he would do this to me, or my family. He must have went thru a lot to find me again. "Oh for God's sake stop it! He's a doll!" A smile escaped as I thought about him, (My Robert was magical you know!) I could hear myself saying these words when I was a little girl. No! I would never blame him, this was much more than he was capable of, this was so much more!

I called my friend Donna it was decided I would talk to our minister. I was somewhat embarrassed by it all as I felt he would ridicule me. She informed me he had actually dealt with demons a couple of times in his career. She would make the appointment.

Things quieted down again. I prayed the rage I spilled throughout my house was enough to keep them away. The appointment was made, and the appointment was broken as a snow storm hit and we found ourselves snowbound. The lights flickered on and off as the wind, snow and now hail raged outside. Something hit against the screen door, then the sounds of scratching and loud guttural cry. I closed my eyes and prayed silently that it wasn't starting again.

The boys ran to the window and looked out, I opened the door just in time as a big gust of wind and snow blew in covering me! The boys laughter filled the air as I was caught off guard. Once I could see again hanging on the screen was a very large black cat!

I had developed a kind of protective phobia against cats, I hadn't been able to attach myself to any cat, after what had happened to my precious cat. However it didn't leave me heartless. I opened the door as the cat jumped down and ran into the warmth of the house. It was a beautiful long haired black cat. My husband dried him off and the kids gave him some food. I had never seen the cat before, it was strange it picked our house. I left the boys to play and took a shower. The cat followed me down the hall staying so close I tripped over him. I couldn't seem to make him go away. When my husband came into the room the cat arched his back and hissed at him!

He couldn't get one step closer to me. The cat seemed to glare and he growled. It had suddenly changed to something sinister. He was a very big cat, his teeth razor sharp and he didn't mind showing them! He was so friendly when he dried him off, now he could tear him apart!

Very odd behavior. I reached down slowly to pet him, hoping the standoff would subside. He rubbed up against my leg. My husband left the room. I don't know why the cat didn't sense the fact that I had to make myself pet him. He had to sense my reluctance, yet he wouldn't leave my side.

I climbed up on the bed with my book, the cat jumped up beside me. He knocked the book out of my hand and rubbed up against me. I tried pushing him away, I didn't want to make him mad as I already saw what he could do. He got right in my face, his green eyes wild looking. He stared at me. I felt very uncomfortable, I shoved him off the bed. He jumped up behind me, and cuddled next to me. Strange purring came from his throat. I could feel him wiggling around, I tried ignoring him. It was just to cold to put him out.

His purring grew louder, he was wiggling around I turned to look at him. I got the shock of my life as that cat was laying on his back. His arms up as if he were reaching for me. His eyes wild, legs open wide and he had the biggest hard on I had ever seen! Did cats do that!? Was it normal!? I jumped off the bed and ran into the living room. I told my husband to get that cat out now! We came back into the bedroom. The cat still laying and purring and exposed! My husband ran toward the bed and pushed down on the mattress. The cat on its feet now and growling, teeth exposed. What the hell was wrong with that cat!?

I ran to the kitchen for the broom. I grabbed the kids and put them in the bathroom and told them not to open the door. I ran back to the bedroom, swinging the broom at the cat. Chasing him thru the house. My husband opened the front door as he ran out! I never saw that cat again, dead or alive. I had never even heard of a cat doing that before, very weird and humiliating!

That night I could hear scratching, on the window screen. When I looked out there was no sign of life. No footprints in the fresh fallen snow. Noises could be heard throughout the house, and the static of the radio began again!

Another appointment was scheduled, and again broken! I had come down with a mysterious illness. It seemed to come from nowhere. One minute I was cooking dinner and singing along with the radio. The next I was chilled to the bone and spiking a very high fever. Seven layers of blankets covered me and I still shook. I drifted off to sleep, leaving my husband to care for the children. The fever bought on a re-occurring dream, one that has been with me since childhood. It only occurs however when I spike a high fever.

The dream is always the same. I know deep down there is a purpose and a meaning I can't quite grasp. I'm floating in outer space, lying on my back, so peaceful, so calm. Asteroids and meteors are coming toward me, I weave in and out thru space. The moon is spectacular, it is so beautiful and peaceful. I'm alone and I'm not afraid. It's like I belong there, I don't want to wake up. The stars twinkling as if they held a secret making the universe shine, it's not so dark, will I float forever or reach a destiny. Then I wake up, the fever is gone and I'm home in my bed. I didn't know how much time had passed but I was suddenly aware I was not alone. Someone sat on my bed bedside me and touched my cheek. I opened my eyes expecting to see my husband. There was only darkness, no sign of my husband. I sat up and scanned the room. The chills were gone, the fever was gone. I felt great. My husband ran into the room, "Are you okay?" He yelled as he ran over to me. "Yes, I actually feel great." I said. "Why?" "Are the kids okay?" I asked. He shook his head yes then told me he saw a black mass of some kind float into the bedroom!

Another appointment was made, and almost broken! I had to work that night. I worked at a mental facility. We were short staffed that night and the moon was full. The residents were more agitated that night for some reason. it made for an almost impossible night. We had gotten a new resident in, she had been moved from two other facilities for her violent behavior. She was responsible for sending two of our own staff to the hospital on her second day at our facility!

It all started because I refused to give her a soda. Our residents were on a reward program and they had to earn their treats. She had lost her points due to her actions. She was a big girl, probably at least 200 lbs and I was all of 90lbs if that. I stood my ground she became combative. She jumped me from behind and started beating me in the side of my head. I somehow was able to twist around, trying to block her blows. I was not allowed to hit her, we continued to wrestle and I ended up on top restraining her arms in between mine. There was only three of us working for 75 residents, and we were all girls! I yelled for the restraints and pulled her to her feet. We reached her bed and I held her down on the bed, while the other two restrained her. I was very bruised and sore, I could hardly move and she had pulled my hair so hard. I knew how the settlers must have felt when they had been scalped! It felt as though my hair were separated from my scalp and it burned so bad.

Another attack or another resident having a bad night would not be good. I could barely walk as she had jumped on my back knocking me to the floor. My knees were bruised, my face beaten and bloody, my earring ripped from my ear. Hand full's of my hair missing, I had been scalped so to speak!

It all began to make sense. Each time an appointment to see the minister was scheduled something prevented it! It was all to clear, it would go to any means to stop me from going! I made it home that morning and with the help of my husband and my friend Donna was able to keep that appointment.

After all we had endured and the beating I had just took, we arrived safely, regardless of the heavy snow that decided we hadn't had enough. The minister said the same thing, he worried each time we canceled. It would stop at nothing to keep me from talking to him. He listened to my bizarre story, I only told him of what had been happening at the house. The rest was a bit personal and I didn't know how to tell him the evil was in me as well as with me. I just couldn't have it scaring my family!

He proceeded to tell me about cases he had been involved in and how things could go terribly wrong. What the problem was, started long ago, I left still unsure as to what to do. I had already stood up to it which he advised me to never do again. I had also prayed and rebuked it. I didn't want things to get worse. He told me to pray and show no fear, hymm already done that. All that stood in my way and all that tried to stop me, that was the best he could do!? I was on my own just as I had always been! I headed home defeated and forever haunted.

I decided I would ask Tina to schedule a time that I may talk to Bren, maybe she could in someway at least shed some light on what was going on with me, the house and the entities that were my life. I was saddened to learn she had suddenly passed away! I felt bewildered as I wondered if it was another way of stopping me from trying to discover what was going on. I felt all hope was gone and I would just have to deal with it. I promised myself no matter what, I would go to any length to protect my family!

THE HOUSE IN THE COUNTRY

I had many dreams of this big white house in the country. It was on a long curvy road and sat on a small hill. There was always a black cat sitting in the window. The swing hung from the front porch and would sway back and forth as if someone were sitting there swinging. Funny thing about the swing there was never anyone sitting there and there didn't seem to be any breeze.

I could see myself walking down the lane with whom I thought must have been a friend, however I could never see her face regardless of the sunshine that surrounded us. We were probably in our teens in my dream. We must have been coming home from school as we carried books as we walked laughing and talking. Then silence when we rounded the curve just before the house. It was odd we would always stop talking and the laughter would seize at that very moment. Then in the blink of an eye, I would be inside the house, alone, and confused.

I would be just standing there in the middle of the room. Seemingly to wait for something. The silence would break, the footsteps would come loudly running from somewhere in the house. I would feel confused and everything would start to move in fast motion. The colors of the room would run together and turn into a kaleidoscope. I could sense the coming danger, my heart would pound with each step as the footsteps grew nearer.

I would start running around the house, upstairs and back down as though I knew there was no other way. The doors and windows seem to disappear! It was just me and the loud footsteps running up and down through the enormous house. Closer and closer they came as I ran and fought for each breath I drew! Room after room no hallway as each door opened into another room! The last room revealed another door that led down a narrow back stairway down into darkness, then a small narrow passage, thru a small hall and finally the kitchen. Then through the house and back up the stairs I would run repeating each step like a broken carousel! Going around and around faster and faster, everything spinning out of control!

Then just before I felt I would pass out or it would pounce on me, the dream would end! To tired to fight, defeated and alone I would wait. It would never come as I slumped down onto the floor of an upstairs closet. The dream was always the same, every detail always ending the same way. My perpetrator never revealing itself to me, yet making sure I was aware of its presence!

I knew in my heart the dream had significant meaning, something lay in wait and someday I would have to face my fears or face the danger I ran from so long ago. Many years later, I would actually live in the house that haunted my dreams as a kid.

We always wanted to live in the country, grow a small garden, give the boys a place to be boys and of course add a dog or two. We found the house listed in the paper. It sounded like everything we wanted, and it was in the country! I made an appointment to see it that afternoon.

As soon as we rounded the curve, a familiar feeling came over me. When I saw the house it all came back to me! The swing on the front porch, the black cat sitting in the window, the eyes that seemed to watch us as we pulled into the drive. I told my husband I had had a dream about the house.

He smiled, I didn't have time to tell him every detail but I managed to describe the rooms. I'm pretty sure he was thinking "The house of my dreams" as a positive thing. I on the other hand wasn't quite sure if I even wanted to go inside. The door opened and a very friendly woman stood there. Two little blonde headed boys, peeked out from around her legs.

She invited us in. the kitchen was just as I told him, the dining room was just off to the left from the back door. The basement was off the kitchen and a pantry on the other side of the kitchen. The large living room took up the biggest part of the downstairs. A door opened into a small hall leading to the bathroom and one bedroom. The staircase was just to the right from the front door a few steps up, a small landing, then the remainder of the stairs.

At the top of the stairs a small landing and a closet right in front of the stairs. Beside the closet was a small bedroom and behind the stair case a larger bedroom. To the left was an even larger bedroom. The house was built in the 1800's so I guess it was normal back then to have several rooms leading one after another, separated by only a door. Giving the effect of a never ending room. This was the space that led to three more bedrooms.

When we entered the last bedroom, I stopped, there was no door for an exit. I was puzzled, a house that large should have more than one escape route, shouldn't it? I stood there studying the back wall. The lady looked at me and said "Are you okay?" My husband was looking at me as well, with a questioning look.

I smiled and said, "Did there used to be some sort of door leading to the kitchen from here?. She looked surprised. "Well, yes there was. Do I know you?" She asked? I said "No, I was just thinking there should have been another way out that's all."

She informed us that her friend used to live in the house. When she was a child she spent many hours playing in the house. The stairway had been sealed off many years ago, but she didn't know why. When her friends parents moved to Michigan, she rented the house, she loved it as much as they did.

She also told us several people were interested in it, and to be honest their income was larger than ours and she was pretty sure they would get it. We didn't have any credit at the time and they did credit checks. We were also told they would do a home visit unannounced as they wanted to make sure the house would be taken care of.

We thanked her and left, never really expecting to hear from them again. We pulled out of the drive way. I looked back at the porch, the cat had not moved, the swing swayed back and forth. I said, "That house wants me." "if we get it, its because of the house, it really wants me".

My husband gave me this look, not sure what to think look. I had described the house to a tee. I had never been there except in my dreams, yet I knew it so well. How was it even possible? He just smiled and shook his head.

When we arrived home the phone was ringing. I wasn't really surprised to hear the woman on the other end say "You got the house!" I stood there as I shared the news with my husband. I was kind of excited but, at the same time I wasn't sure why! I told my husband "I told you it wanted me, there will be a showdown, I don't know why but there will be."

We moved in a few days after that. The house was so big and beautiful, we didn't really have enough furniture to fill the house, and winter was coming. We decided the bedroom at the top of the staircase and the one on the other side both facing the street would be our best choices for now. The boys loved it, there was so much room.

We made a play room out of the first room that opened to the other rooms. Several rooms were nailed shut and the knobs were taken off including the closet in the now toy room. The owner still had a few things in there as well as the room beside the closet at the top of the stairs. It too was nailed shut with no knob. The house was huge and more than enough room for us and then some.

When the weather started getting colder we decided to make our room where the dining room was. The kitchen was so very large that it not only accommodated our large table but also our hutch. The dining room was just perfect for our bedroom. The smaller bedroom was perfect for the boys and the living room was so large the boys had space for toys and a good space to play as well.

We were happy there, and the dream faded as all seemed to be perfect. I worked the midnight shift at a development center for the mentally handicapped. The shift worked well as the boys were in bed when I went to work and were just getting up when I returned. They didn't miss me that way and they were safe with their daddy making my job a lot easier.

I came home that Sunday morning, cooked breakfast of pancakes and bacon. Got the boys ready for Sunday school, cleaned up the kitchen, kissed them and sent them on their way. Now for a relaxing bath and a nap before they get back. It was an hour to and from church and at least a two hour service including Sunday school. I had three hours to myself.

I bathed and cuddled up in the soft warm blankets sinking into the comfort of my waterbed. I was so relaxed nothing could invade my sleep as I closed my eyes.

Without warning out of now where, I was caught up in a nightmare! I could see the house, the dream from my youth all over again! The black cat sat in the window, the unseen presence swinging silently back and forth. The footsteps so loud and yet, never seeing who I am running from.

165

My heart was racing, I knew something was different this time. I was in pursuit, I was tired of running. I knew why I was there, and yet I was confused. I sprang from the bed and ran to the stairs. I could hear the footsteps, so loud, so close. I started up the stairs, but before I could take the first step something covered my head. I struggled with it, it was a blanket! Then came another and another. I was throwing them back up the stairs as fast as it was throwing them down! Then came the curtains one right after the other.

I could hear the banging on the closet door! I could hear the footsteps as they seemed to run from the room to the stairs, so thunderous the entire house seemed to shake. I could hear growling, and smelt something not so pleasant.

I continued throwing the blankets and curtains back up the stairs. I was getting nowhere. Each time I tried to run up the stairs to face my childhood demon the more the battle continued! I could hear my parrots chirping in fear. Their cage was on the first landing as you went up the stairs.

The blankets seemed to be some sort of mask, it would not allow me to go up the stairs. It would not allow me to see! What was it trying to tell me? I didn't understand why blankets!? I was sweating and out of breathe the blanket was over my head again I fought with both arms trying to get it off! Something grabbed me as I fought I came to my senses when I heard a familiar voice!

"It's okay baby I've got you!" I fell into his arms, I was totally out of breathe. He held me for a while, my heart still racing as I struggled to gain composure.

"He said, "That must have been some dream!" "You were standing in the middle of the bed fighting with the blanket over your head!" He said. "Yeah, I guess so, but it was so real"! I began telling him my dream. It had been so real a few minutes before, by telling him, I could begin to laugh it off as just a nightmare.

The boys came in a few minutes later and asked if they could go upstairs and play. I told them it was really to cold, but they could bring more toys down. They ran up the stairs, and right back down, yelling "Mommy, Mommy, there are blankets everywhere, the curtains are torn down and "Mommy all the doors and the closet door is open!!!"

I jumped out of bed and ran for the stairs, my husband close behind me. I ran up and yes indeed it was as the boys said. The blankets were every where, the curtains had been ripped down off the rods and shredded. There were toys all over the floor. The closet door was wide open! The closet door with no knob and had been nailed shut!! The doors to the other rooms that had also been nailed shut with knobs missing were also open!

I couldn't have possibly done these things, I used to walk in my sleep as a child, but even if I had thrown blankets everywhere and toys and even went so far as to rip my curtains off the windows. I couldn't have possibly opened the closet door, no knob, nailed shut, NO WAY!

My husband looked at me in disbelief, we sent the boys downstairs with their toys. We searched everywhere for a screwdriver, a hammer anything that could give us the answer to the open doors. Nothing anywhere. We picked up the blankets and shredded curtains and headed downstairs.

The boys were at the landing looking into the bird cage. "Mommy, something's wrong with the birds." Fearing the worst, we told the boys to get some ice cream and go play in their room. The parrots lay at the bottom of the cage. Both dead! Tell me how two healthy parrots, playing and chirping hours before just end up dead! I remember hearing them in my fight, the fear in their voices the fluttering of their wings, their fear.

I knew I didn't do it, I couldn't have done it! I told him the house wanted me. I warned him there would be a showdown. It just didn't make sense. I was at a loss, I still even though I knew it must have been a dream. It just wasn't really possible, for it to not have really happened. The evidence was clear, the meaning however, still laid beneath the blankets that kept covering my head. Hiding under a mask, not quite ready to reveal its true self, or meaning.

It was done with me for awhile, playing the endless game. Leaving a piece of the puzzle buried somewhere deep within my memory, forever digging into my soul, leaving me to wait until the next time, never knowing when or where and probably never knowing WHY!

SOMEWHERE THE ANSWER LIES

Even though we had the house blessed things continued to happen. The kids and I were alone and vulnerable, secluded at times and often snowed in. My husband was back and forth in the hospital, sadly many lonely dark nights awaited us. Shadows made their presence known occasionally and footsteps were heard as they seemed to dance across the ceiling. Doors seemed to slam shut regardless of the fact they were nailed shut! The morning light would come and I would venture up the stairs expecting to see the doors open. I was only a little surprised to find they stood solid, nails in tack, just the echoing of the bangs rang out reminding me of the night before.

We loved the old house regardless of what was happening. I was no stranger to the paranormal, It's just I had never had a direct encounter to the extinct of this. It was almost as if the house was trying to make me remember something that occurred in my dreams long ago. Perhaps it was a thought planted in my head by the memory or dream of someone I used to be, "If you believe in that sort of thing"! I tried searching my soul, wandering into the depths of my own childhood. Searching for any sort of validation that I may have been there before. Maybe we knew someone that used to live there. Each time I came up empty, no, I had never been there in this life.

The remembrance was buried deeper than that, unfortunately the owners decided to sell the house, even with everything that went on there, I was accepting what it was and determined to solve the mystery which surrounded me. It was more room than we would ever need, but if it were ours we would make good use of every single inch of it. The owners were getting up in age and wanted cash, something we did not have. It was sad to say good-bye especially since I felt so much a part of the house. I felt the answers were perhaps hidden deep within its walls and it would eventually come to the surface given the right time.

Alas, just like always I was given a small piece to fit together the puzzle which was my life, only to realize the time was not yet permitted. The missing pieces were not yet coming together. I may never know how to fill in the gaps. The house wanted me, now it was willing to let me go, was I getting to close, to soon? There was nothing I could do about it, my time here was up, the house sold and we had to move.

The odd part about the selling of the house came with a knock on the door one winters evening. The snow had just started, its large flakes falling gently from the sky. Funny how something that light and fluffy could cover the earth in such a short time. Quietly sneaking up without making a sound, it was just beautiful. The man and woman stood on the front porch, smiling as I opened the door. They announced they had just purchased the house!

We had not shown the house to anyone, it was hard to believe someone would buy a house sight unseen! The really odd part was the girl seemed to know me! She called me by name and told my husband we were friends in junior high, as she ran over and gave me a hug, saying it was so good to see me again! She was a stranger to me, I had never laid eyes on her before! Even when she told him her name, no spark of remembrance came to mind. I have searched my mind even to this day, I do not or never did know her!

Was she also summoned to this house, as I was? Could it be she was the one who walked with me in my dreams. Were we both a part of something we couldn't imagine, was it her turn to fight with the thing inside. Was she the answer to what bought us here? Did she also have the same dream as I? Was it the dream, our friendship was based on? Funny now that I think back I never saw my friends face as we walked the country road just before the house came into view.

Every time the house came into view, she was gone, and I was alone in the house with what laid in wait! A thought has come to mind that perhaps, something happened to her, was that what I was supposed to remember? Was she actually even here? Or worse was something going to happen to her!

Was I somehow summoned first, to draw her here? After all in the dream I was separated from her, alone and she was nowhere to be seen! Was it really her the house wanted? Did we have to come together in the dream to cause the reality we were now facing! Should I have warned her!? What did I have to do with it? Did I witness something horrible, was she the victim? Did something happen to both of us?

It was an odd situation, I had so many questions, but it was just to creepy to discuss. Besides I didn't know where to start. Maybe she had a lot of secrets, and missing pieces, searching as I but not ready to reveal. I decided to just let it ride, besides maybe she wasn't ready, after all it was her that seemed to know me! Maybe she already knew the answers and was waiting for me. Truth was I had zip to offer! It still bothers me, not knowing who my friend was, and why the house. To many variables, too much to think about, to many unanswered questions. It was clear the time has not yet arrived!

I only hope nothing bad happened to her or her family. She after all knew me, maybe she would remember something. Something wanted her, it wanted her enough she bought the house! Then again maybe she hadn't yet remembered anything, but me! Would she remember in time! Funny that most of the time when you see someone that supposedly knows you, eventually it will come back to you. Some recollection of knowing them and their names will eventually set your mind at ease. Especially since we were supposed to be friends. It blows my mind that all these years have since passed and I still do not know who she is!

I drove past the old house a while ago, I was shocked! The front porch was gone! No swing, no black cat, no sign of a once beautiful two hundred year old home! It was ruined! They had enclosed the entire front of the house. It was a horrible site! I didn't know what they had done inside, but I think she must have gone mad!

How could anyone do this to such an historical beautiful home! It stood out like a sore thumb, so hideous and cold. It wanted her, maybe she was strong enough, maybe she won, destroying the house the only way she could. Perhaps the house did her in, causing the madness that is now what stood before me.

Somewhere the answer lays, maybe it's in plain sight, just within reach and I am blinded by its truth.

THE TROLL

I only saw her once, where she came from I will probably never know. The moon shown through the window, it was so bright that night. There was no mistaking what I saw. She stood there frozen for a time. I could feel her presence, thick and strong. It was clear, she was blocking the door. She wanted to make sure I saw her. Regardless of her attempt to alarm me, her efforts failed. I knew I should have been frightened but truth is she didn't frighten or unnerve me although I don't know why.

I don't know where she came from, or why she came, nor where she went. I do know I saw her just as plain as day. Although, it was only the moon light that shone thru the room, I could see her so clearly! She stood there in front of me, starring at me face to face. We were so close I could touch her. I will never forget her, maybe that's all she really wanted, just to be remembered.

A lot of things had happened in our lives and I was trying to give my children some stability after the passing of their daddy. Times were hard and we were scared, sometimes it just seemed impossible to go on with life when so much of me had died when he did.

I wanted to pack up and grab my children and shelter them from everything. At the end of the day in my heart I knew rebuilding our shattered lives was what I had to do.

It was in the spring when we first entered the house. The children ran from room to room exploring each room, the slamming of the door indicated they had went outside. Bonnie the home owner had left us to wander and roam on our own.

The house wasn't large but had three bedrooms, the neighborhood wasn't great but the payments were more than affordable. I was at a loss I just didn't know if it was the right decision and I had no one to discuss it with. I stood alone in the middle of the front bedroom, which was the largest of the three. I heard footsteps behind me felt a soft hand pat my shoulder.

I turned my head to look at what I thought was my son only to find I was alone. I knew at that moment I would buy the house. It was as though I had my answer with the pat on my shoulder a little reassurance he was still looking out for us.

The house was a mess, but it was do able. The down payment was made and the papers signed. The boys and I worked on the house for three weeks getting it ready for move in day. The night we moved in was my first mistake. The neighborhood turned into a crazy reckless, hell bent experience!

The quiet shady neighborhood by day was inviting, however at night all the crazy people came out! Cops everywhere! Gun shots broke the silence of the night. Neighbors fighting with one another. Families arguing! What have I done! No money to move on, I would just have to make the best of a bad situation! I spent nights pulling the kids to the floor when gun shots rang out. It was pretty rough the first summer we were there. Fortunately winter came and the violence came to a stop!

I would notice little things now and again, but with my past history of spirits I dismissed it and went on about my business.

My sister, her children and my mother came to live with us the following year. Fortunately the neighborhood was a little better, but still had some undesirable tenants that would move in now and then. Since they rented they never stayed long mostly because they didn't pay their rent!

My sister noticed things around the house, noises here and there, shadows, footsteps, feelings of being watched, at times uncomfortable not really knowing why. She, like me never mentioned it until the night (the troll) came.

My sister shared a room with her daughters, the bathroom was located in the bedroom at the time. I had gotten up to use the bathroom in the wee hours of the morning. So I wouldn't disturb them I tiptoed thru the room and quietly opened the door. The moon was pretty full that night and cast such a brightness through the room that there was really no need to turn on the light.

I quietly opened door, to find her standing there blocking the door! She stood about my height perhaps a little taller making her about 5ft tall. She was husky built with thick arms and legs her face was rather full and she had dark sort of curly hair that reminded me of an ratty old wig. Her dress was flowered with rather large flowers, old and a bit dirty. Her face held a greenish glow of sorts and she was covered in large warts. She just stood there staring at me. The moonlight shone on her as plain as day. There was no mistaking she looked so solid! I didn't feel afraid even though I was trapped in a small space and there was clearly no way out but thru the door.

I didn't want to wake anyone so I just stood there. Taking it all in, she was very hideous looking and a part of me felt sorry for her. I finally just put my hand in front of her face to push her away and she just disappeared!

I stood there for a second not knowing where she went, curious, a little confused, but, shrugged it off and went back to bed. I slept well that night.

The next morning I started breakfast the kids were in the living room watching television. My sister sat at the table with my mother drinking a cup of coffee. She lit a cigarette, then broke the silence. "Well, did anyone else see that ugly thing in my room last night?"

I continued fixing breakfast pretending not to hear her. She again asked "Did anyone see that ugly thing in my room last night, well early this morning like 2am?" Before I could say anything she said, "I know you did'! "Now how did you make her disappear?"

I turned to her and said, "What did you see?" I just wanted her to verify what I seen. Make it more creditable that I had seen it. With the morning sun, last night had been put out of my head for a few minutes. After all I had had many things happen before so one more thing was just that. One more thing.

The kids came in about that time so our conversation was put on hold for a few minutes. Once the kids were feed and outside playing the topic was once again priority. She wanted an explanation. Mostly I think to make sure we saw the same thing! For her own sanity she needed to know. I asked her "What did you see?"

"It looked like, for the lack of a better word an old troll!! That thing had warts all over its face black with a greenish kind of glow flowered dress, thick built, a little taller than you." "That thing was f-ing ugly!!

Mom just looked up from her coffee cup and laughed. My sister said "Don't laugh I saw that thing and so did she!"

I said "Were you afraid of it?"

She took a hit off her cigarette, looked at me and said "No". "I really wasn't, but I don't know why".

"I don't know if it was because you weren't alarmed, and when you just made it disappear and walked away like nothing happened, I was more confused than anything else." "How did you make it go away"?

"I'm glad you saw it." I said, "It's always better when someone else witnesses for themselves."

Mom looked at me, she also wanted to know.

"I think it was just instinct, I was trapped in a small area, I didn't want to wake anyone up. I just automatically held up my hand and put it in her face, I was going to push my way thru!" "She just disappeared right at the same time!"

"I just don't know where she went, I've never seen her before."

Funny thing is none of us ever saw the troll thing again. However it's strange that my sister has seen a woman wearing a flowered dress run from the middle bedroom through the kitchen area several times throughout the years. She has yet to see a face. She says she runs very fast blending the colors of her dress like watercolors running down a canvas.

So could it be that the troll thing appeared as a troll to get our attention. Did something happen to the one who runs through the house? Is the troll thing careful to not allow us to see its face again? What does she want? Why is she here? We may never know. But then again she may make another appearance when the house is quiet and the moon is just right!

MESSENGER

I was working at a small family restaurant not far from my home. I was the only waitress at the time, the restaurant could accommodate fifty two people. We had a limited menu with daily specials so it was a breeze even when we were busy. We were only open for breakfast and lunch, it was an ideal job for me as I could drop the kids at school and pick them up when school was out.

The restaurant was doing fairly well so we decided to expand the hours. We decided to try a dinner menu, I was to help them get the night business and then go back to days as I wasn't a fan of leaving my children at the mercy of babysitters. It was slow getting it up and running.

The restaurant was located in a strip mall only problem was there were very few stores open in the area. Most just couldn't make a go of it, so the shops sat cold and empty.

It was around seven on a cold winters night. It was dark outside with only a lonely street light to glow over the almost empty parking lot. I watched as the snow fell silently on the ground. We had had two customers since five o'clock and all they ordered was coffee.

I started wiping up and preparing to close when two men came in. One was an older man, medium build, probably in his mid fifty's or early sixty's. He was very well dressed, dark wool trench coat, dark suit and tie. His salt and pepper hair was very clean cut, regardless of the fact it touched the tip of his shirt collar. He donned a wool black rimed hat, and although he wore very dark glasses, it didn't disguise the fact that he was blind. His cane was also black and the strides of his footsteps coincided perfectly with each step he took. He was very sure of himself and seemed to be a professional of some sort.

His partner although a little younger, tall and lean, also well dressed and clean cut. His brown wavy hair somewhat longer than his companions, hung loosely over his brow. They both wore cologne and although both were different fragrances, they seemed to work together. Their scents filled the restaurant as they walked thru.

I greeted them and smiled as I poured hot steaming coffee into their cups and ice water in their glasses. The blind man seemed a little uncomfortable and I noticed concern in the younger man's face. I handed a menu to the younger man and recited the specials to the blind man.

I walked away giving them time to decide what they wanted. I returned a short time later. Before I could ask if they were ready to order, the blind man spoke. His voice was a bit quiet, his tone had a smooth and gentle quality to it. He spoke very clearly with a sense of urgency in his voice.

He surprised me when he held his hand open and said, "quickly dear, give me your hand!" I glanced at the younger man as he nodded his head.

I placed my hand in the palm of his hand. Although he had just came in from the cold his hands were warm. He covered my hand with both of his. I for some odd reason felt safe. Something I hadn't felt in a long time, but that was short lived.

He although blind, looked up at me, as if he wanted to remember me. He wanted to see me. See inside my soul or something! His once kind looking face changed, a peculiar look came over him, his mouthed quivered. He looked terrified!

I was confused by his sudden change and very disturbed when I realized he was terrified of ME! I had managed to make a blind man see and I managed to screw the beauty of that brief moment of sight he had by terrifying him!

What could have been so bad that he was so clearly shaken with fear! He jumped up practically pushing me out of the way with his cane. "I have to go!" the other man looked as confused as I, but fear also covered his face. He shot a look at me as if to say, "What are you!"

I was confused. I said "What's wrong, at least tell me what you see!" They pushed away from me and quickly exited the door.

I sat the coffee pot down and followed them I would demand an explanation! When I reached the door I was surprised to find no sign of the men any where! Furthermore I looked for footprints in the snow so I could trail them. There were none! No sign of anyone having been there at all except for the coffee cups.

They could not have just vanished into thin air! They couldn't have been ghosts, his hands were gentle and warm and solid! What had just happened! I had a clear view of the parking lot even if somehow they jumped over the snow, which would have been impossible. There were no tire tracks! Where did they go!?

Were they some kind of messenger? Where did they come from, and why didn't he tell me what he saw! Were they ghosts!? I still to this day don't know what it was all about and why they came. I certainly don't know what the man saw, but I do know what fear looks like, I saw it on his face that night.

As I locked up and confirmed the existence of the two men by the cook, who thank God did see and hear them. Otherwise I would probably have thought I was in the twilight zone or something. I thought about my life, and wondered what was in store for me after the blind man invaded my world.

I locked the door and headed for my car which now sat alone with the snow covering all but the silhouette of its structure. I sat there a few minutes my hand was shaking as I put the key into the ignition and started the car. I glanced around searching desperately for the two men, I knew it was useless but I had a glimmer of hope.

What had he seen! What evil was awaiting me!? What evil was inside me?!

Did he know about the Mantis Man? The Moth Man? My Robert? The Man in the closet? The Teenager? The Devil Doll? The Plaque? Was it the strange words I chanted from the plaque that night? Did he know about the Blood Stone? Did I seal a deal with the Devil himself while I was under hypnosis? Is that possible?! And if it were, would it have been a sealed deal since I had no control over it!?

Or was it something else? Did he know what happened to me the night I left the apartment and was gone for so long. Did he know where I went and why? Did he know about the dreams I had throughout my life? Was it all a part of something so terrifying that I sent them fleeing into the cold, dark snow covered night?

Did he flee because there was and is no hope for me?

Could he not have pulled me to my knees and prayed for me? Wouldn't God's blessing over me have saved me!? Saved me from what I am or would become or will endure. Do I hold the key to disaster?! Will God reject me when I need him? Am I dead to him? Did I even have a chance? Was I destined the day I was born, marked by an unseen darkness!

Or was it something else? Something so horrible I have yet to encounter? Something so horrible no one can even begin to imagine!?

Whatever it was it was enough to send the messenger back to where they came! Leaving me confused to say the least and wondering what evil they saw in or around me! Furthermore wasn't it his duty as a Seerer to warn me of evils yet to come! Even if I wouldn't have believed him, shouldn't he have warned me!?

For days I searched for him. Asking everyone I came into contact with if they knew or had heard of him. It was if he never existed. I never saw either of them again.

I remember that night so well, his presence still haunts me to this day. I think about the messenger and wonder if it had all been some kind of crazy dream. His face forever seared into my head, his words haunting me forever. The terror I saw on his face, I can never forget. I after all caused a blind man to see beyond the darkness of his sight. Down into the bowels of hell to pure evil! I didn't even get the chance to tell him I was sorry he missed the beauty of life.

I didn't even get to thank him for making me feel so safe when he held my hand. Now that I think about it, I probably made him feel dirty and could very well have caused him nightmares forever.

Perhaps somehow, the tables were turned. What if the moment he touched my hand I became the messenger! Was I some sort of vessel depositing disaster and horror into the world with a simple touch of my hand? What message could I have portrayed to send the receiver fleeing from the warmth of the restaurant into the cold darkness.

Perhaps, I have it all wrong. Was he a messenger from the dark and I a saint? Perhaps he received a surprising message from me to all evil that God still is very strong and will overcome all evil!

I recalled words whispered behind my back throughout my life. "She's an evil child" She's not from around here, she doesn't belong here." 'She's very mean, you can see evil around her."

Then the other side "She's a disciple." She's an alien princess." She's a healer." "She has been here many times before." "She is gentle and caring."

Then "Things seem to happen when she's around, she knows things."" She scares me! She doesn't seem to be afraid of anything!" "you dare not make her mad!"

Then there it is, the big question "WHAT'S WRONG WITH HER!"

Perhaps the messenger received a message from me. One that will haunt him forever as well as the Omen he left for me!

"FOREVER HAUNTED!"

THE CONVENTRY OF WITCHES

The first time I went to witches circle was in the summer of 2000. There was a chain stretched across the path and the tree nearby held the warning sign of "No Trespassing". I remember how warm the night was and how very dark it had became in such a short amount of time. Eyes seem to follow us every step of the way. It was a heavy thick feeling we knew we weren't alone by any stretch of the imagination.

We had gained permission to investigate the cemetery by the trustee and the sheriff's department. We promised to report damages and anyone doing ill deeds that we may encounter.

The cemetery was a walk into the woods around a slightly curvy path. The cemetery had a history of practices of the occult and being hidden in the woods was the perfect spot. It was very sad to see the condition of the stones as I stepped onto the holy grounds.

The cemetery was rather small but held several stones and debris of what was left of stones that were vandalized by uncaring people with little or no respect of the sacred ground. Legend had it that a woman had been deemed as a witch and therefore her husband forbid her to be buried inside the cemetery with the rest of the family. She instead had an unmarked grave outside the cemetery.

Witchcraft and practices of the black arts were held inside the grounds along with animal sacrifices. The cemetery is formed into a circle with rows of stones scattered throughout the circle.

We entered the cemetery and spread out getting a feel for the place. The air grew thicker and the night seemed to grow darker.

It had an eerie feel to the area, and unexplained noises were heard coming from somewhere just outside the circle.

We did an energy circle and EVP and snapped several pictures. I was the last one to leave the area and followed the dark path alone back to the car. I snapped several pictures for light as my flashlight was always the one thing I hardly ever carried. Although it is a vital part of being in the dark, I find I would rather carry equipment that could bring evidence instead. I depended on the flash of my camera to help light my way.

Of course ghosts or spirits are known to drain equipment and believe me I've had my share of darkness due to these conditions, but, nonetheless I still depend on it. As I walked the path my camera failed, surprise! I felt a presence behind me and heard footsteps somewhere behind me. I turned but the darkness shielded what followed me.

It soon began to play with me, camera came on camera came off. Although I did manage to see my way down the dark path to the others, I wasn't able to capture my playmate regardless of the many pictures I took.

When I reached the chain across the path the others were there waiting. I stepped over the chain and felt something pull me down. I couldn't get up it was as if something held me down. It wasn't hurting me, I began laughing as I tried getting to my feet, only to be pulled down again.

I described the feeling to the others, it was like I was magnetized and a giant magnet kept pulling me down. One of the girls tried helping me up, she too could feel the energy around me. It was if they didn't want me to go.

One of the other team members started taking pictures, I was surrounded by orbs and finally I was set free.

It was awhile before I returned back to the cemetery. It was actually pretty funny how it all took place. My friend Joyce and two other girls decided to go to the cemetery. We all knew the risks of what we were doing but we were excited to see if we could capture whatever held me down last time I was there.

We met at the gas station Sonya led the way and Joyce and I followed. When we arrived we parked our cars on the winding curb and got out.

As we stood outside the chained entranceway despite the darkness that surrounded us the warning sign stuck out like a neon sign "No trespassing". The air was somehow different and seemed to have a special warning for us. We all felt it. The vibes were undeniably, very strong. Kathy suddenly spoke "witches circle, four of us, witch of the east, the west, the north and the south".

Once the idea was planted, we stood there deciding if we should go into the woods. About that time we heard a dog barking somewhere close and getting closer to us. We heard a strange noise somewhere in the woods behind us. We looked around for the dog. His barking was getting closer and closer to us. We started moving towards the cars watching for movement as the barking suddenly stopped.

Joyce, Kathy and Sonya were at the side of Sonya's car while I was at the back rear fender. It was very quiet now and they stood beside the car as I peeked around to see where the dog was. To my surprise the dog was looking right at me! I said, "He's right here!"

Everyone scrambled to get in the car. Once inside we all started laughing at our predicament. I was in the back seat in a baby's car seat while Sonya was next to me in another baby's car seat! Kathy was in the passenger's side looking like someone had thrown her in while Joyce was in the driver's seat!

Ironically Joyce was the only one of us who didn't drive! The night was just to weird, extremely dark, strange vibes and the dog. We decided maybe better trust our instincts after all there were four of us and we all had the same vibes.

The next time we visited it was with a larger group. The walk thru the woods was not unlike the others. The woods seemed to close in on us and eyes seemed to watch as we headed down the path.

I was always drawn toward the far back of the cemetery, near a declining hill and the creek. A few stones lined the hill. We had been there for quite awhile when a couple of people started to get a little uncomfortable and wanted to go. My friend Joyce experienced a magnetic force that seemed to give her problems keeping her balance. She described the feeling as some sort of magnetic field pulling her to the ground. The same force I felt on my first trip to the circle.

Joyce ironically is a descendant of one of the women that was accused of witchcraft at the Salem witch trials. Perhaps they were trying to keep her with them.

We finished our EVP sessions and last minute picture taking. As usual I was the last one to leave the cemetery. I stood at the back for just a few more minutes. I really wasn't ready to leave, I felt as though the activity was just about to begin.

One of the guys waited at the entrance way and shot one more photo in my direction. We left shortly after that.

A few days later I received a call from the guy who took my picture. He said after viewing the pictures he came across mine. I was hardly recognizable. My face looked skeletal but the thing beside me was what really captured his attention. It was a hooded creature, standing right beside me!

It was standing as though it were watching them and somehow protecting me! Could this be the same force that held me down on my first visit. What would have happened if we had stayed longer that night! He gave me a copy of the picture and when I blew it up on my computer I was amazed at the creature.

It was not human, yet wore a hooded robe. Its mouth was open as if it were screaming! Was it some kind of witch, a demon, I didn't know but given the fact it was so close to me standing beside me seemingly to scream and stand its ground with me was definitely creepy. Was I mistaken as someone else? Or, perhaps I looked like one of their witches of long ago.

Whatever the case may be I didn't feel threatened or afraid even after I saw the picture. It was just a little bizarre to say the least!

I went back a few times after that trying to find the entity again, but only the feeling she left us with remained. The last time we went my sister had gone with us. Although still no sign of the creature it left its mark.

My sister had broken out with a very strange rash. We thought maybe it was some kind of poison ivy, oak or sumac. She was very uncomfortable with it and had a low grade fever accompany with it. She finally went to the Doctor as it was getting worse. I teased her and said it was a witch's curse of some kind of crud. After all if it had been any kind of poison, I would certainly gotten it, as I am very allergic to the elements.

She was after all in my corner of the cemetery more than any other area. She to felt the vibes of the area. Funny thing was the Doctor had no clue to what it was! I told her she was branded or warned not to return. At any rate she has never been back since!

It wasn't to long after that we were sitting in our hotel room having dinner. Something kept hitting my hair lightly. At first I thought it was a fly or a spider or something. I swatted at it a few times. Then I felt something heavy cover my head. I turned to my sister and said is something on my head?

That's when I saw the sides of a hooded cloak as if I were little red riding hood. The cloak had a gold silk lining and the hood was a kind of dark hunter green velvet material. She didn't see anything and as soon as I described it to her it was gone!

I couldn't help but remember the hooded creature and all the things related to the witches circle. Was I an unwilling participant of a coven of witches so long ago and was somehow recognized as one of their own!

I thought about another cemetery where I was with two other girls and our picture was taken as we sat by three stones of babies. Boils appeared on the picture covering our faces. Was this also the works of witch craft, to protect what was now gone.

I also thought about the cemetery down the road from witches circle. Something inspired me and I started dancing around. It was not yet dark and the sun was warm on my face as I spun around magically like I had no control of what I was doing. It just felt right somehow. Funny how things come together. When I snapped pictures I was surprised to see the stones looked as though they too were dancing! It almost looked like a wedding party of long ago!

Something happened to me that day several pictures were taken of me as well. It was if my body were somehow "leaving"! One picture revealed my lower jaw looked like someone else trying to enter.

When I arrived back home I started feeling really sick for no known reason. I got into the shower to cleanse myself of any unwanted spirits. I couldn't shake the feeling until I finally looked into the mirror and said in a very stern voice. "Get the hell out of my body"!

I started feeling better and the effects of that day lessoned, however, every time I do scrying I see her, and the others. Sometimes I think she reminds me of an old Indian medicine woman, her face changes sometimes her eyes glow and she reminds of an eagle getting ready to soar. Sometimes her face looks almost like a lion or some kind of cat. Her face changes again from old to young and none look like me and then my face will sometimes disappear. The last time her face looked as though it were melted or scarred from burns, perhaps burnt as a accused witch on a stake!

Who is she? Is she my spirit guide when I see the old Indian side of her? Is she merely an old hag that has invaded my being? Is she from a Coventry of witches and I somehow am a part? Are the others here with her as well? What are they trying to tell me?

What am I? Who am I?

What message is she trying to convey to me, is it a link to a past so long ago that I don't remember, is she trying to tell me who I am and where I finally belong! One thing is for certain she is getting stronger and isn't afraid of showing herself to others as they too have seen her.

The hooded creature has not been seen but the hood that was placed on my head and shoulders was unmistakable. I saw it, felt the heaviness of it, am I a member of a Coventry of witches!

I know where she came from, I do not know her name. I know I must take her back. But what then? She has been with me for awhile now and won't easily return. What will happen if I go back, will she resist, will she fight? Who will be there to help me if indeed I need help?

What if that is just what she wants me to do! Is it a trap? Do I really want to know who I was and what I may become!

I guess it could explain a lot of things that have taken place over the years. There was a time when it seemed animals were destined to my house, where they just seemed to die suddenly. Someone made the statement that I must be a white witch. The animals are sick, I was told and they came to my door for me to heal them.

I was worried about west nile fever when fourteen birds fell to their deaths in my yard. I called the health department, I was told there was no threat and no reports in the surrounding area. I questioned my neighbors and they had no problems of dead anything's in their yards.

That was just the beginning. a few days later a rabbit was stretched across my drive way, dead, no apparent reason. Later in the week a dead cat lay just a little under the back porch. Then followed by the death of a squirrel.

Then more animals came, two groundhogs sun bathing on my back porch! A raccoon bravely knocking at my back door all hours of the day and night. Aren't these animals supposed to be nocturnal? Several other cats started hanging around, one trying to get inside my house thru a screened bedroom window. Then two opossums actually getting inside my house! It was definitely a crazy time.

Strange looking spiders were in my bathroom. I have never seen spiders like them before and I haven't seen any sense. There were two of them seeming to travel together. They were very large and black. Their legs looked very strong and were very long. They didn't crawl they jumped! Then came the cricket spiders odd looking creatures, they still come from time to time.

It could also explain the mysterious things that happen to people that have done me wrong. All I have to do is say "get em"! Something takes over, protects me, takes care of me, it won't allow anyone to do me harm in any way, without getting even or leaving them with a warning. I hope the warnings they receive, will not go unnoted or something worse could happen! I must not be a very good person, but, I really mean no harm! For I am Forever Haunted.

THE PRESENCE

Lately I feel the earth move under my feet. I can't seem to (shake it) if you will pardon the pun. It has been more and more frequent and no one else seems to notice. I really don't know exactly what it means, I just feel it is some sort of vibration under my feet like a vortex of some kind waiting to erupt or perhaps waiting for some sort of opening that I am supposed to allow or cause in some way.

It started after my investigation of a home in Indianapolis, Ind. I was in the shower the very first time I felt it. I jumped out thinking although rare it must be an earthquake, it shook very hard I could barely keep my grip as I scrambled out of the shower! I flung open the door to find the floor now solid under my feet and my sister sitting on the sofa calmly reading a book. I said,"Didn't you feel the quake?"

She only looked at me as if I were nuts and replied there was no quake, at least I didn't feel it if there were. I called downstairs to the front desk to inquire about it and see if anyone else had reported anything of it, and later the news nothing at all was my answer.

Since I had been personally attacked after the investigation and it wasn't the first time while I was "In the shower" I had to chalk it up to another attack. Only thing is It's still going on. I must have hit the core to whatever lays in wait or something.

May 26, 2012 I felt a very strong presence several times that morning, the earth shook as well only this time was different. It was accompanied by waves of nausea, I was disoriented as well as confused. It was as if I were being separated from myself. When I stood up it was the earth shaking, confusion, nauseated disorientated mess. When I sat down I could still feel the earth shake and the presence around me.

This lasted for what seemed like a very long time but in reality probably only a few minutes at a time, but, continued on for most of the morning. When I went to the front desk to run a report I sat down in front of the computer. I was talking to the front desk agent when the phone rang, she went to the front part of the office to answer it. I started my report when I felt a presence behind me, I figured it was the agent so I continued to work. I heard a man's voice behind me, it was very clear and very audible, it was very close to me. There was no mistake in the words he spoke, he clearly wanted to make sure I heard him. His words were "I love you"!

This of course caught my attention as I knew there was no one at the desk but the two of us. The agent was still on the phone taking a reservation. I looked everywhere just in case someone had came in, which I knew in my search I would find what I already knew, no one else at least that I could see were there.

I left the office and started down the stairs to my office. I felt very weak and shaky my head started pounding and my heart started racing, I didn't think I was going to make it to my office before I collapsed. I finally reached the bottom of the stairs before I realized what was happening to me. Once I cleared my head I whispered out loud, "Who are you"?"!!

I darted to my office, I felt better but still a little nauseas and still could feel the earth shake at times. I was to leave at 2 o'clock that day for an overnight hunt in Ohio. In view of everything that had happened to me that day, I admit to having second thoughts of going. Only because I thought I was going to ruin the trip for everyone as I still didn't feel right.

I'm not one to back away or let my friends down so I decided I would go on with my plans. I was either going to face what had happened alone or with others that could help me understand what was happening.

Maybe it was a warning for me not to go, or perhaps knowing that I would, it was somehow a forewarning to an opening of a past I would soon encounter.

As it would turn out something had indeed erupted from a childhood past so long ago. No one could have known as I never spoke of it to anyone. Right place, right time, right combination of people we all had to be there to somehow reunite my past. Although I still don't understand why "Ohio" as I didn't really grow up there, from childhood anyway. Metaphorically I have stated I grew up on the streets of Dayton, but it was in a way of being able to take care of myself, a real eye opener so to speak. So I have to say somehow the people that were present that night was prevalent in the timing.

In view of everything that happened that night I have to wonder if it is him that has watched over me all these years. Protecting me, keeping me safe. At my beck and call without me knowing, after all it would make sense when I think of my very first friend, my very first love, and it all started so long ago in kindergarten.

ROBERT COMES TO LIFE

I think sometimes the right setting and the right people just have to be together. They have to be present at just the right time for certain aspects of the past to come to full circle in the present.

It all goes back to my theory of everyone we meet there is a reason for it. I met my friend Kristyn several years ago at a hotel I was working at. She along with a group of paranormal investigators had come to check out our own haunted hotel. We seemed to make a direct connection and understood each other almost immediately. I had of course had my own ghosts long before I got involved in her group. Time never stands still for anyone, several years later she quit the group and went her separate way.

I stayed awhile longer then in order to grow felt the need to find myself going solo.

I guess you could say I out grew the group, they didn't seem to want the same things as I did. I wanted to reach out more to people that needed help, and wanted to do something with the information I was able to obtain. I didn't want to do an investigation knowing people were afraid and merely say "You have ghost, good luck with that!"

I wanted to help them, make it go away give them their lives and homes back. I didn't want them to be afraid anymore. I would not let them face it alone, I wanted them to know I cared and wouldn't just leave them. I can say I learn something every time and I know in my heart I have done just what I vowed to do, and that is to help where ever I can. It was the best thing I could have done for myself and my quest for the unknown.

Kristyn eventually joined another group we still remained friends and I eventually joined her group sorta. I now have my own group and somehow we merged together. We travel together to many locations and investigate many homes and businesses. We work well together and enjoy each others company and input. They are a great team as are mine, together we get the job done. It helps that we have a wonderful demonologist that makes himself available should we run into trouble.

We were on location at a rectory somewhere in Ohio. There were several of us, some I had not yet had the pleasure of meeting and working with for the first time. I can imagine that they probably thought I was a nut case. However, the events not only took me off guard but stunned Kristyn as well as the others.

Although I have been friends with Kristyn we rarely get the chance to just sit and talk about anything. We are usually on an investigation or a hunt somewhere and that is our main focus. We rarely talk about our lives, which makes it very interesting when we are together. This is not the first time an event like this has happened to us. It's almost like we just have to be together in order to complete a full circle in a paranormal way. I don't understand the location, but perhaps the right people were all present at just the right time. Maybe we all had to be together to bring the event to life for what ever reason. Perhaps there is a hidden connection we have not yet discovered.

We were in the basement doing EVP. It was very dark down there and smelt musty. There was an old mirror on the back wall. Kristyn and I sometimes will do scrying if we feel something around us. Some of the other investigators had not heard of scrying before and soon became interested to see how, and better yet, if it actually works.

They were eager to learn more techniques and were really amazed at their discovery.

Scrying a technique also called crystallomancy, it is used by seers, psychics, and people like me to communicate with the other side. It creates a doorway for communication. When you look into a mirror or any reflective surface even water it acts as a doorway so to speak. This allows you to "see" not only visual contact but often verbal as well.

It is known to intensify psychic energies. Sometimes more than one spirit tries to come thru and that is why we are able to see our faces change so many times. The more dominate one usually wins over and takes center stage.

These things may be in an attempt to answer a question you have asked. Some may be confusing and not make sense but may have a significant meaning to someone else.

We stood in front of the mirror and held our recorders always hoping to capture EVP. It wasn't long before our faces started to change. My face went from an old Indian looking woman to a young woman to no face at all, while Kristyn's face went from evil to sinister to an old troll then to a face where the features were distorted and somewhat mangled, some said they thought it looked melted as if it had been burnt or something. A face only a mother could love!

We decided to do an EVP session. Kristyn is unique in a way that sometimes spirits will communicate thru her, she has the ability to see sometimes and sometimes just knows things but doesn't know where the thought comes from.

I can sometimes see them or events of things happening, sometimes I see things before they actually happened and am very confused and arguementive that it has already happened. I have also at times felt their pain. Neither of us can make these things happen, they sometimes just occur out of nowhere and we have no control over them. They don't happen all the time and we don't have any warnings before they occur. It just is what it is, we can't change it. One thing is for certain we work well together and things seem to happen when we are together.

I started off with who are you? The spirit using her for communication came on without warning. It was like someone else was using her thoughts, she simply said "YOU KNOW".

I then asked what is your name? She answered "YOU KNOW.

I asked again, "What is your name? "I don't know you." The reply was confusing as she spoke again, this time the words came out stronger and matter of factual insisting 'YOU KNOW"!!

I could tell the presence was male but I didn't recognize the face. I didn't "know" him at all. There was no recognition of any sort coming thru. I still didn't feel just right but I couldn't blame it on this as it started prior to my coming. Then again it had everything to do with what was going down!

The face in the mirror was so distorted and seemed to hold a sadness so deep within it's soul. I felt an unusual connection for some odd reason. I could almost cry as I felt the deep sadness and bewilderment of his pain and loss, but I had no idea why. He seemed to be searching for something or someone for a very long time.

Again what is your name? The reply was the same insisting "You know" this time more long and drawn out. Almost as if he were prompting me to search my own memory for a clue. The darkened room seemed to be closing in on me as he kept insisting that I knew!

Once again I said "I don't know you!" "Tell me who you are!" this time my voice was quieter, more refined. I felt overwhelmed with thoughts that rushed in and out of my mind, nothing really making sense. I felt bewilderment for the entity that looked back at me.

I kept looking at the face in the mirror, so sad, yet no reconnection crossed my mind. I tried envisioning what he would have looked like minus the mangled melted features that would haunt my soul forever.

I demanded "Tell me who you are, I don't know you!" When he finally spoke thru her I was speechless! She simply said "ROBERT"!

I stood speechless shaking my head no. I finally found the words that were even as I spoke, as unsure as I was sure I didn't know him. I guess a part of me when he said Robert knew him and it took me back many, many years. I just couldn't accept it. It's a trick I told myself! A spirit playing with us.

For a brief moment flashes of a long lost friend flooded over me, it was just not possible I told myself.

I said "Robert, you're not my Robert."

"Yes I am" she replied.

"No, you are not my Robert!

"Yes, I am! She spoke in a very firm voice!

"No, you don't look like my Robert, you aren't him!"

"Yes! I am!" She shouted!

"Then show me, you don't look like my Robert. Prove it. What are you?"

In a down hearted forlorn voice "Just dust." was his reply. His words hit home, my heart sank, as even though he must be my Robert he was nothing like him as I remembered.

"Robert!" I said I'm a shaken, yet excited and still a little unsure voice. It took me a minute to absorb and reason with myself. Was it after all possible?

We got into a lot of trouble, I said. His reply was "Yes, we did!"

"I looked for you, I'm sorry I couldn't find you."

"They took me." He said matter of factually.

"I know" I replied in a very quiet voice. I shook my head in disbelief. A part of me couldn't accept the image that looked at me from the mirror. The words he spoke through Kristyn, she couldn't have known about any of it! It was just too bizarre! Could this really be "Robert, my Robert!" The Robert that was so loyal and loving when I was a child! The one who found me throughout the years. Is this what is left? Was I the cause of his demise, was it after all my fault?

Would he find his way back to me in a few years? Would he forgive me, for not taking better care of him? I hated myself for losing him again. I walked away not knowing what else to say, I was so sad and stunned at the same time. I knew the people that were a witness to this madness, probably thought I was crazy! It would have been hard to watch and not think we made it up. I was surprised when I turned and they were as quiet and somewhat stunned as I.

The questions began, first one then the other. They were concerned and interested. Not thinking for one minute what they had witnessed was anything but the truth. They knew Kristyn, trusted her, was a friend to her. When she turned to me and looked surprised, they knew it was real! I simply said, "You wouldn't believe me if I told you!" I said in a quiet sober voice.

"Yes, we will, you have to tell us who Robert is!?" they prompted. Reluctantly I told my story, of my faithful friend and how we met in kindergarten so many years ago. I told them how he seemed to search for me throughout the years. As fate would have been written for me we met again, the chances were slim to none. It had to be fate. I told of the last time I saw him and about the way he was taken from me. I had lost him forever it seemed, and yet, the thing in the mirror insisting he was "My Robert!" Was a bit more than I could accept.

He wasn't the same, his smile was gone, he didn't look anything like my Robert, I just wanted to cry. Cry for the child I used to be, cry for my "Robert" I longed to hold him again and feel safe. He made me safe and protected me, I didn't do the same for him. I was bewildered, and I prayed I would see him again. Not the hideous thing in the mirror, but my Robert with the turned up smile and bright eyes that stole my heart. The Robert of long ago, the one I could recognize, the one I loved so much, the one that loved me!

I wanted to hurt the ones responsible for hurting and destroying my Robert. I wanted to make them pay for what they did! Truth was I didn't really know who did it, I had no proof. I was heartsick; I knew my only hope was that "Robert" being my magical "Robert" would over come this! He would find his way back as he always did! He just came to me to see if I still loved him, missed him, wanted him. He would return, I know this in my heart. I have to believe he's not really gone. He's just waiting for the right time to return! Perhaps we go back to somewhere in time, many centuries ago. There after all has to be some connection for our strange encounters and love for each other!

HAS IT ALWAYS BEEN HIM

As I put this book to bed, I thought of all the things in my life, the uncertainty, the everyday things that became normal to me. The harsh words that were spoken against me because I was "Different." The constant reminder I was somewhat not normal. Always being the last anyone thought of, but the first to blame! I recalled later in life, being told I was a witch, I was evil, I didn't fit in, bad things happen when "She's around!" I didn't want to be bad and I didn't want them to be afraid of me! Couldn't they see I was harmless!

Then the total opposite, I was a disciple, a guide, a sensitive an empathy. A physic in the making, not living up to my potential. A white witch, a ghost witch. Then to the extent of checking to see if I was in the book! When I inquired, I was told if I was in the book I would be accepted! The only book is the book of knowledge, or the Akashic records, when I mentioned them, they said they would get back with me! Well I guess I was "In the book" because I was asked to help with certain paranormal cases, mostly pertaining to the darker entities. "Yay, me!" how did I get so lucky! Just when I thought I wasn't all bad!

Then I thought of my first protectors, the ones that kept me safe. My mother was the very first, she alone in that snow bound house pulled me from the safety of a certain death. She defined all odds against her, little did she know what came with me. I often thought had she known what I would become, would she have fought so hard to keep me? Then my Grandpa, who would love me no matter what. The one who made me feel special regardless of what I was and would become. He always said I was special, and I guess I was to him. Was he wiser than he knew? Could he have known what I would become?

Then the one or ones that refuse to let me be hurt by others. The one or ones who come to my aid in the most unsuspecting ways. The one or ones I call "KARMA!" funny how when I would get really upset because someone did deliberate harm to me, all I would have to say or think was two simple words. "GET THEM" and It wouldn't be long until all hell would break lose! I never really wanted to cause harm to anyone, I just want them to know what can happen, a warning so to speak. I just won't be bullied or pushed around anymore, by anyone! "KARMA" has my back, it's out of my control mostly, what happens I mean, I just need to be careful what I say!

My Robert was the first to be my special friend, he took care of me through kindergarten. He has found me throughout my life. I have to wonder if we were lost to each other somewhere in time long before I ever knew. It would make sense after all. I recall him telling me stories of castles and such. Then the dream I had of dancing with an unseen presence. The surroundings were in a large ballroom of perhaps medieval times, judging from the gown I wore. I remember feeling his arms around me as we danced. When I felt him becoming to close I would turn and start to run away. His hand would touch my hand and I would melt back into his arms as we danced.

The dream continued, him to close, me running away, then back to him again. Never seeing who danced with me. Just feeling his gentle touch, I could see me dancing all around the ballroom. The chandelier casting shadows as we danced. We were alone, the music was soothing and I seemed to be under his spell. When I awoke the next morning I could still feel his arms around me, I could still see us dancing as I dressed for work. It was like I was watching a movie. I couldn't break away from it, maybe I didn't want to. It was very alluring, hypnotic a trance like state. I remember telling my sister what a beautiful dream and I couldn't wake up from it. Ironically it was a dream I had a few days before I would once again reunite with "My Robert!"

I have to accept the probability that perhaps he is my protector! He has always been with me. He just appears from time to time to let me know he is near. Perhaps he has loved me throughout my entire life and maybe even before! Could it really be possible "My destiny, my life, forever tied from a past I have yet to discover. Could it be and has it always been "My Robert!" "My Protector!" "My KARMA!" After all "My Robert is magical you know!"

ALL I HAVE TO SAY OR THINK IS GET 'EM

Through the years I have been gathering an Army of sorts without even realizing it! Everything I have experienced in life and made to endure was merrily a process of my destiny. I have been protected by unseen presences throughout my life. It seems all I have to say or think is a simple slip of the tongue, "Get 'em". Something is watching, waiting for my instruction. I don't really understand what my destiny is and how far these unseen beings are willing to go to protect me. I don't understand why I am the way I am. I have many questions, many concerns. I mean no harm to anyone really, but I am thankful that something protects me.

Many people that have done ill deeds to me have met "Karma". A name I have given my protector. Karma can be brutal, Karma gets the point across. Karma takes names and recalls bad deeds against me by others. Karma awaits my command, sometimes Karma acts on its own! Karma at times is out of my control I know I was meant for something bigger than I can imagine it's a little scary as I pray it is not for evil doing. I was marked, when I was born. Followed throughout my life. I am supposed to know, I suppose when the time comes, what the extinct of my deeds will be.

So many times I have wondered if I was just pure evil. There is what is called the Askachic records that hold the names of some. Also the book of shadows and the book of knowledge. I do not understand the meaning of its contents. I was told I was in the book. I was accepted, yet I never applied! A deal must have been made long ago, that I innocently fell into. I have been told I am not from this world. I don't belong. Maybe I have been sold into something to free someone else's soul. So many encounters that have been a slight more than witchy.

Then there is my Robert that has found me throughout the years. Perhaps we were together in another realm of time. Perhaps a curse was placed on him, turning him into a doll. Maybe I was supposed to undo the curse, I failed miserably! So many encounters with spirits that seem to know me on the other side.

I'm too comfortable at times in the craziest surroundings. I don't have the good sense to recognize the fear that I should feel. Maybe in a sense I am to trusting of the things I don't understand. I thirst for knowledge, beyond what is tangible. I cross boundaries that I should run away from. I fear no evil, maybe I am of God. But I fear I am something darker than the night. I can't seem to help who I am. I have been chosen in a sense, to a destiny I have to fulfill whatever the cost. Maybe I wear a mask, I don't think of myself as truly evil. I want desperately to unveil the real me. But I fear I will not like what I see.

I know what your thinking, I see things that are yet to come. I feel things from long ago. I come from the past, the present and the future, in a sense that I experience those things at times. Déjà vu is commonplace, I grow confused at times when the past catches up with the future. Haunting me more so, when the present takes me back to the past. The future is masked at times giving me just a glimpse, but protecting me from seeing the results until the ordeal happens. It makes me so angry sometimes that I can't stop or prevent things from happening. It leaves me sad and empty, yet yearning for more. It leaves me alone at times and forever haunted. Forever and ever.

CARDS ON THE TABLE

Well now that my cards are on the table, I know you are scratching your head and saying out loud, "What a crock of shit!" I don't blame you, it's hard to accept things you may have never experienced. This book was written believe it or not, for my own sanity! Yes, I finally can face the childhood plaques of my life! It makes for an incomplete puzzle, but it is also a start! I don't really care if anyone believes, I know what happened, I know how I felt, I know what I've seen. I wanted it to be my imagination so many times. It would have been easier to accept. It would have been nice to have had a friend that understood me along the way. Someone somewhere to guide me, teach me, make me more aware of what was happening to me, make me embrace the knowledge I was born with.

I could have put my experiences to good use. Sad part is after my friends read this book they may look at me differently, I may be alone again as I have been most of my life. My family may abandoned me, but "Karma" will always have my back!

As it is now I have just had to deal with things on my own, gathering bits and pieces and getting a piece of the puzzle a little at a time. I will continue to write of my life, my investigations and hunts as well as experiences on locations as well as my own home. I will continue to follow my destiny where ever it may lead me, for I know nothing else except I was put on this path for a reason. I can only hope and pray it is to help and send lost souls to the light. I can only hope and pray I am not the evil everyone will fear as my destiny draws nearer!

We all have our demons to face, our hidden memories, maybe I've given you something to think about! Maybe I've even inspired you to write about your own childhood memories! After all they may not be as innocent as you think! Go ahead, I DARE YOU! Face your demons! It's the only way to sanity after all.

I look into the mirror at the image that looks back, so empty at times, so dark, yet my aura is surrounded by light. I look into the eyes of a haunted past, a haunted future and I accept my destiny, I will forever be "FOREVER HAUNTED"!

Printed in the United States
By Bookmasters